The 20% Leader

Strategic Execution for Leaders Who Want to Move the Needle and Win Back Their Time

Paul Lange

Manolutions Publishing

First Edition 2025

Contents

Foreword By Paul Lange

This book wasn't written to impress anyone.
It was written because it had to be.

Over three decades ago, I became a financial founding partner in a private equity and venture capital firm—joining as the youngest gun on the partner team. At the time, I had minimal exposure to the world of structured finance, venture deals, and capital markets. But what I did have was hard-won experience in scaling businesses, optimising operations, growing teams, and increasing asset value—earned through building and exiting my first company via a leveraged buyout with the help of my mentor.

That background became my edge. While learning the financial ropes, I was also hands-on with our portfolio companies—working directly with leadership teams to drive clarity, execution, and commercial outcomes that lifted enterprise value.

After that exit, I went deep into the work—coaching and advising leaders inside companies, from lean startups to multi-million-dollar enterprises. Different businesses. Different industries. Same frustration every time:

They didn't need another framework.
They needed **focus, leverage, and real traction.**

The idea for this book came over 30 years ago, when my late mentor pushed me to write down the systems I was using in the field. I didn't.

At the time, I didn't feel I'd earned the legitimacy to write it.
Yes, I was delivering results, but something held me back.
Years later, client after client pushed me again:
"Put this in a book."

Not for inspiration.
For access.

The 20% Leader is the result.
Not theory. Not fluff.
Just the part that actually moves the business.

This book draws on my **Total QX methodology**—a high-performance operating system that integrates clarity, prioritisation, leadership alignment, and engagement into a single coherent framework. I don't name it on every page. I don't need to. You'll see it in the way each chapter cuts straight to the point and translates vision into velocity.

This isn't a mindset book. That will come later.
This one is the **missing half**—the part most books leave out.
The part where you **take action**, reset your leadership rhythm, and move your business forward.

So, if you're expecting another long-winded read full of motivational metaphors and half-baked leadership philosophy, you're in the wrong book.

But if you want the edge—
The cut.
The clarity.
The confidence to execute faster and lead sharper ...

You're in the right place.
Let's get to work.
- Paul Lange

P.S. If you're looking for the mindset side of the equation—visualisation, alignment, energetic clarity—that's coming next. This book gives you the execution edge. The next one sharpens the inner game.

Individually, they both work. Together, they compound.

I wrote this one first for a reason: after working with hundreds of leaders, I found that mindset shifts rarely stick until action happens first and waiting for perfect alignment before moving just stalls progress. But once someone starts taking action—even messy, imperfect action—it clears the path for mindset shifts to land fast and stick hard.

That's why this book leads with execution. It gets you moving with precision.

And once you're in motion, the mindset work doesn't just make sense—it amplifies everything.

This is the part most leaders miss or misfire on. They either skip it entirely—or execute without clarity, without traction, without rhythm.

Avoid that mistake.

Nail the action. Then sharpen the mind.
That's where the real acceleration kicks in.

Lead first.
Align fast.
Multiply everything.

Foreword By Thomas Power

I've known Paul Lange for over two decades—since the early days of Ecademy, when a few of us dared to imagine a future where business was truly personal, community-driven, and led from the heart, not just the head.

Paul stood out back then, and he stands out now. A natural leader with relentless curiosity, commercial acumen, and a deep sense of human potential. Over the years, I've watched him move seamlessly across continents, industries, and boardrooms—coaching, investing, advising—yet always rooted in one mission: to make leadership clear, sharp, and impactful.

This book, The 20% Leader, is not just another addition to the leadership shelf. It's a field manual for those brave enough to lead with clarity and act with speed. It's the antidote to the slow, bloated, over-complicated leadership models that so often paralyse progress. Paul writes the way he speaks—direct, intelligent, no fluff. Just the truth, told clean.

What makes Paul's work exceptional is that it lives in the real world of business. His Total QX methodology isn't theory—it's forged in the pressure cooker of venture-backed deals, private equity boardrooms, and real-time operational challenges.

He's not offering you platitudes. He's handing you a blade to cut through noise and find focus.

If you've ever felt overwhelmed by complexity or stuck in a leadership fog, this book is your signal flare. It will remind you that clarity is leadership, that real execution begins with bold prioritisation, and that teams don't follow vision—they follow belief.

Paul, my friend, you've nailed it. You've captured what we all need right now—momentum, not management.

Read this book. Keep it close. Then go lead like you mean it.

Warmest,
Thomas Power
Founder, BIP100
Professional Networker, Advisor, and Friend

Note from the Author

Please read this first—even if you skip the 'About the Author' page.

This book was written for leaders who value clarity over clutter, sharp thinking over shallow noise, and results over rhetoric.

What you're holding is neither a summary, nor an oversimplified repackaging of complex ideas.

It's a precision tool. I've stripped away the fluff, cut the bloat, and distilled decades of leadership, coaching, and execution strategy into something you can use now.

Fast. Clean. Effective.

You won't find long-winded theory or padded chapters here. What you will find is a clarity-led, momentum-driven framework that helps you focus, prioritise, and execute at a level most leaders never reach.

If you're wondering—yes, the name *The 20% Leader* draws its inspiration from Pareto's Law. But it avoids the trap of being another 80/20 book. There are libraries full of those.

This isn't about observing the 20%—it's about becoming the 20% that actually drives results. That's the difference.

Underneath this book is the **Total QX methodology**—a performance framework I've developed through decades of leadership coaching, business optimisation, and accredited leadership and management training. It's the foundation behind everything we do at Manolutions, and it fuels the thinking in these pages, even if it's not always named directly.

Now, I want to be upfront. This is the *only section* where I speak directly about our services. There's one brief mention again on the final page—just to make sure you have a clear next step if this book struck a chord.

But that's it.
No pitch. No funnel.
Just value.

If you'd like more information, head to **manolutions.com.**

Whether you lead 5 or 500, your job is to cut clutter, drive clarity, and be the ultimate True North—so that your team delivers results aligned to the company's goals, values, and strategic direction.

Your leadership determines whether productivity gets boosted or busted, whether profitability is real or just a myth on a spreadsheet, and whether the asset value of the business grows—or deflates faster than a virgin after his first home run, only to be berated for finishing too quickly.

Because execution doesn't care what your title is.
It responds to the sharpest signal in the room.

Finally, if you're someone who wants deeper insights, more tools, and the backstory behind this book's creation, a more detailed edition is in development. But this version?

This is for the leaders who want sharp edges, clear moves, and fast traction.

Use it. Lead with it.
And most importantly—**execute.**
– Paul

Acknowledgements

Thank You, Heinz (RIP)
— With Gratitude and Respect

This book has been a long time coming.

More than 30 years ago, my late mentor encouraged me to document the frameworks I was using—sharp, field-tested, results-driven. At the time, I didn't feel I had the legitimacy to write it. Yes, I was working with leadership teams, optimising businesses, driving serious ROI—for us as investors, and for the founders too—but it didn't feel like enough.

Years later, I was told by countless clients:
"You've got to put this in a book."
Not for vanity. For **access**—
so more leaders could benefit, even if they never worked with me.

This book is that answer.
It's lean. It's punchy.
It's only the stuff that actually drives execution.
No fluff. No filler. No theory.
Just the 20% that actually moves the 80%.

To my late mentor, and the many past clients who pushed me to write this:

Thank you.
This book exists because of you.

Gratitude to Thomas Power — A Visionary Leader Who Made the World Catch Up

A special thank you to Thomas Power for contributing the foreword to this book. I've known Thomas for over 20 years, since the early days of Ecademy, which he co-founded with his wife Penny Power OBE back in 1998. Born in a pizza shop in Farnham, UK, Ecademy was the world's first online social business network—preceding everything we see today, including LinkedIn and the entire era of social business networking.

Thomas is a true pioneer in the business world, with all the best qualities of a leader—vision, generosity, and bold execution. His long-standing commitment to empowering business owners at all levels—from startup founders to enterprise leaders—has influenced millions globally.

He also coined the now well-known distinction between ORS (Open, Random, Supportive) and its opposite, CSC (Closed, Selective, Controlling)—a powerful lens for understanding modern leadership, digital transformation, and the rise of value-based, network-centric business thinking. It remains one of the most enduring and transformative contributions to how leadership is practiced and trust is built.

Today, ORS thinking has quietly embedded itself across networks, generations, and cultures—shaping how people show up, connect, and contribute, often without ever knowing its name.

I'm honoured by his contribution to this book.

To Thomas Reid — A Living Example of Leadership

I'm always grateful for your friendship and the presence you bring. You are a living example of what it means to lead from the front.

You've always embodied the highest principles of leadership — not just in what you teach, but in how you live. The world needs more of that.

Our conversation about working with purpose and precision within two solid, effective hours stuck with me more than you probably realise. To this day, I continue to iterate and refine it as a personal benchmark.

To Bob — For the Philosophy Forged in the Final Third

Thanks to my good mate and cigar-and-rum co-conspirator, Bob Meguyer.

Some of the most revealing insights don't come from workshops or whiteboards but show up in the final third of a good stick and the last sips of great vintage rum—when the world quiets and the truth shows up at the end of a hell of a lot of real talk between mates.

Philosophical. Practical. Tactical. Unfiltered. Often in territory few are wired to explore and most aren't ready for. You've been there for those moments—and they've mattered.

To JJ Ferrari — The Nudge That Rekindled the Fire

Thank you for the very firm nudge—it landed. Whether you meant it as a spark or not, your words helped reignite this project and bring it fully to life. You show up bold, real, and unapologetically true. That kind of presence shifts people. It certainly shifted me.

Thanks Jennifer for the Real Talk and Conversations That Cut Through

Thanks to Jennifer Fiedler for many deep conversations that opened a window into the film world—and its unapologetic approach to getting things done. What began as a post-networking exchange became an unexpected contrast study, and collaboration in execution: the raw accountability of production deadlines versus the padded excuses of corporate delay.

Different world. Different standards.

Execution on set is instinctive—driven by pace, precision, and performance. These guys and gals eat pressure for lunch, dodge punches when they have to, and make corporate "urgency" look like a white-collar neurodegenerative disorder.

What passes for crisis in corporate is their SOP.
It's what they train for—every day on the job.
Pressure in the boardroom? That's just Tuesday on set.

It's a great reminder that leadership doesn't live in titles—it shows up in the result.

To My Son — The Real-Life Test of Leadership

To my son, who challenges me daily—not just with questions, but with presence. You push, test, and reflect back more than most adults ever will.

Through homeschooling and beyond, you've forced me to grow—sharper, stronger, and more aligned.

Every lesson I teach, you return tenfold in perspective.
Every leadership principle in this book? I've had to live it with you.

There's no room for theory when you're watching—only modelling—and while I don't always get it right in the moment, every challenge you throw my way makes me better. This book has my name on it. But you're in every line of it.

To My Wife — For the Long Game

It's forged through friction, tested by contrast, and held together by shared commitment—especially in a world where tapping out has become the norm, where walking away is easier than walking through, and where quitting gets dressed up as self-care.

Most marriages expire faster than phone contracts. Longevity is treated like an accident—not a choice. Discomfort is too often confused with incompatibility. Ours has never been scripted. It's been real. It has lived the same truth this book is built on—when the mission matters, pressure doesn't break you.

An enduring marriage is a masterclass—in patience, perseverance, and showing up even when it's hard.

Who This Book Is For

This book is for leaders who don't have time for fluff.
For operators, founders, and execs who are already in motion—and need to sharpen what's next.

Whether you run a tight five-person unit or lead a 500-person division, The 20% Leader was written to help you drive clarity, accelerate execution, and move with authority.

Specifically, this book is for:

- ✓ **Operational Leaders**
  who manage teams, deliverables, and outcomes—and want to raise the standard without burning out.
- ✓ **Scaling Founders**
  who need leverage and rhythm, not more hustle and chaos.
- ✓ **C-Suite Executives**
  who are sick of watching good strategy die in a swamp of vague ownership and blurred accountability.
- ✓ **Emerging Leaders**
  ready to shift from being the one who executes to being the one who drives execution.

If you're responsible for outcomes—and your team looks to you for leadership—this book will hit.

Not with theory.
With tools. Rhythm. Leverage. Precision.
Because *title doesn't make the leader*—execution does.

Introduction: The Clarity Catalyst

Most leadership books are bloated with fluff. This isn't one of them.

This book is about execution. Not just getting things done—but making damn sure the right things get done. Fast. Decisively. Without micromanaging or second-guessing every move your team makes.

That requires one thing most leaders think they have... but don't:

Clarity.

The 20% Leader isn't just out front — they're at the centre. Surrounded by structure and motion. Grounded in clarity. **Driving both foundation and force.**

The Hidden Tax of Indecision

Every day, leaders across the globe bleed time, momentum, and morale—because they're making too many decisions. They're reacting instead of choosing. **Shuffling what matters** instead of setting a clear priority. Spinning plates instead of building machines.

It's not that they're lazy. It's that they're overloaded. Everyone wants more output. So they throw more effort at the problem—more meetings, more reports, more Slack channels, more task lists.

But real leadership doesn't happen by adding more.

It happens by cutting through the noise and creating clarity so strong it eliminates friction.

Great leadership isn't about solving everything.
It's about making sure your team knows exactly what matters—
even when you're not in the room.

Why Most Leaders Are Failing (Quietly)

Let's be blunt.

Most leaders are failing. Not because they're incompetent. But because they're exhausted. They're stuck in reactive mode, trapped by a thousand micro-decisions. They confuse activity for progress. Strategy for clarity. Movement for momentum.

They look productive.
But they're actually just spinning wheels.

The teams they lead?
Frustrated. Confused. Drowning in misalignment.
Everyone's busy, but no one's building.

It's not a lack of effort—it's a lack of execution.
And execution breaks down when clarity is missing.

What This Book Will Do

This book will make you dangerous—in the best possible way.

You'll learn how to:

- ✓ **Cut through chaos** and lead with undeniable clarity.
- ✓ **Set a singular priority that sticks**, even under pressure.
- ✓ **Create execution momentum** without micromanaging.
- ✓ **Build First Follower movements** that carry your vision forward.
- ✓ **Use Micro-Leverage moves** to shift your team into action in minutes.
- ✓ And do all of it faster, sharper, and more effectively than 99% of leaders you know.

You'll stop reacting and start leading. You'll shift from "busy manager" to *20% Leader*—the kind who moves the needle, ignites teams, and builds unstoppable momentum.

The Clarity Model JFK Used to Launch the Moon Mission

We'll dig deeper in the next chapter, but here's the high-level preview: John F. Kennedy didn't launch the moon mission by issuing a 200-page report. He gave a speech so clear, so bold, and so undeniable that it aligned an entire nation.

"We choose to go to the moon in this decade..."

That wasn't a goal. It was a *choice*.
And it changed everything.

That's the power of
Clarity → Clear Priority → Execution.

It's not a framework. It's a weapon.
You'll learn how to wield it.

Why Your Business Should Run Like a Movie Set

Let me ask you something:
Why are movies made faster than most businesses can schedule a meeting?

Because a film set doesn't have time for indecision.
There's a budget. A vision. A deadline. Everyone knows their role.
The director sets the intent, and the crew gets to work. Fast.

No one needs to "circle back." No one's "waiting on alignment."
It's execution, or it's failure.

That's what Jennifer Fiedler calls **The Hollywood Execution Model**—and it's one of the most potent leadership metaphors you'll ever adopt.

What if your business operated with that level of urgency, clarity, and precision?

This book will show you how to make it happen.

Commander's Intent: Leading Without Micromanaging

If the military can coordinate complex missions under fire—without needing 37 Slack threads—you can run a business with clarity.

Commander's Intent is the concept that underpins every effective mission. The leader defines the *outcome*, not the *steps*. The team has autonomy, but it's aligned with the mission.

This book brings that same principle to your leadership toolkit.

What Comes Next

We'll walk you through the frameworks. But more importantly—we'll make them usable.

By the end of this book, you'll have:

- ✓ A working **Clarity Engine** for your team.
- ✓ Tactical tools to apply **Micro-Leverage** daily.
- ✓ A fully structured **30-Day Execution Challenge.**
- ✓ Optional coaching add-ons (only if you want support).

You'll become a ***20% Leader***—the kind who does less, leads more, and drives real results.

Ready? Let's go.

Chapter One

Why No One Knows What's Important

(And Why It's Your Fault)

Your team isn't confused because they're stupid. They're confused because you haven't made it clear what matters. That's the hard truth of leadership. Clarity is your job. If your team doesn't know what to focus on, it's not their fault—it's yours.

The Chaos Trap

Most teams are stuck in a fog of **conflicting and competing demands—each pretending to be the priority**—busy with a hundred tasks, uncertain which ones actually matter. Here's what it sounds like:

- "What's the priority again?"
- "Is this still important?"
- "Didn't we already try this?"
- "I'll wait until I get confirmation..."

Every one of those is a leadership failure.

Not because you didn't *say* what to do, but because you didn't say it in a way that *cut through.*

You're not leading with Commander's Intent—you're drowning your team in ambiguity.

Decision Overload is Real (and You're Causing It)

Most leaders think more options = more empowerment.
That's wrong.
More options = more paralysis.

When your team doesn't have clarity, they default to two behaviours:

1. **Hesitation:** "Let me wait and see what others do."
2. **Overwork:** "I'll just do everything so I don't get blamed."

Both are execution killers.

Your job is to reduce the number of decisions your team needs to take, not increase them.

That doesn't mean controlling everything—it means setting the destination so clearly that *they can navigate without you.*

This is where **Commander's Intent** comes in.

Commander's Intent: Clarity Over Control

In military operations, lives depend on clarity. That's why the military doesn't micromanage. Instead, they use something called **Commander's Intent**:

> *"Here's the mission. Here's what success looks like. Get it done—even if the situation changes."*

It's the ultimate leadership move. You define the outcome. Your team figures out the path.

You don't need to know every step. You just need to make the endgame undeniable.

When you lead this way, you:

- Remove bottlenecks.
- Empower faster decision-making.
- Reduce fear of failure.
- Build trust through autonomy.

Most business leaders do the opposite. They issue partial instructions, change direction midstream, and flood their teams with half-baked initiatives that compete with each other.

No wonder execution grinds to a halt.

Real Example: "Which of These Nine 'Top Priorities' Should I Ignore?"

A VP I once worked with had a dashboard showing nine *"top priorities"* for the quarter.

His team? Completely stuck.

No one could make progress because everyone was stretched thin across competing goals. One project would start, then stall. Another would ramp up, then get paused. Everyone was afraid of being blamed for dropping the ball—so they tried to carry everything.

They were doing *everything*, which meant they were moving nothing.

We sat down and asked a simple question:

"If the quarter ended today, what's the one real win? The one thing you'd own as yours and feel great about?"

In this case, the answer was clear: "If we get the new onboarding system live and fully operational—without delays."

That became the only priority.
Everything else was deprioritised or deferred.
Execution tripled in two weeks. Not because the team worked harder—but because they stopped wasting effort on noise.

Of course, in every company the answer will be different. But the power is in asking the question—and having the courage to act on it.

And here's something most leaders miss:
The word **"priority" was never meant to be plural.**

It entered English in the 1400s as a singular concept—**the first thing**, the one matter that takes precedence over all others. It stayed singular for 500 years.

Only in the 20th century did we start using "priorities," trying to stretch a singular concept across a dozen competing demands.

But the truth still holds...
"When everything is important, nothing is."

Yes, different departments can have their own sub-focuses aligned to a bigger goal. But at the organisational level there can only be **one true priority at a time.**

One unifying focus. One True North. One priority.

The discipline of leadership is being able to name that one thing, and have the guts to say no to everything else—at least for now.

Strategy Isn't Clarity

Here's a brutal reality:
Most strategic plans are so vague they could apply to *any* company.

"We want to innovate faster."
"We're doubling down on customer experience."
"We're building a culture of excellence."

Sounds good. Means nothing.

Clarity isn't strategy. Clarity is *specific*.

It answers:

- What matters *right now*?
- What are we saying **no** to?
- What does **success** look like in one sentence?

Most leaders avoid this level of precision because it forces them to commit. It puts a stake in the ground. And if they're wrong, they can't hide behind strategy-speak.

But this is where real leadership begins—with **bold, accountable clarity.**

If your team needs a PowerPoint to understand the mission,
you haven't done your job.

The Three Clarity Filters of a 20% Leader

You don't need a thousand tools to create clarity. You need three filters:

1. **Outcome Clarity** – What are we actually trying to achieve? (In plain English.)
2. **Priority Clarity** – What gets done *first*? What gets cut?
3. **Execution Clarity** – What's the minimum action required to move this forward today?

When you lead with these, your team stops spinning.
They stop overthinking.
They start acting.

This is the foundation of JFK's Clarity Model, which you'll see again and again:

Clarity → Clear Priority → Execution.

JFK Didn't Say "We're Exploring Space Innovation"

When JFK announced the moon mission, he didn't mumble about innovation or say "we're looking into space travel." He said this:

> *"We choose to go to the moon in this decade and do the other things, not because they are easy, but because they are hard..."*

There's no ambiguity. No waffle. No bullet points.
Just *clear, purposeful commitment.*

And what happened?
Teams aligned
Budgets flowed
Timelines locked
Execution exploded

Whether you believe the U.S. actually landed on the moon or think it was all filmed on a soundstage in Burbank doesn't matter here.

What's undeniable is this:
The speech worked.
It aligned a nation.
It created movement.
And it gave people a reason to act—without needing more instructions.

That's what happens when a leader stops trying to say everything—and chooses to say **one** thing, *powerfully.*

Choose, Don't Decide

There's a key distinction we'll keep coming back to:

Decisions react to conditions. Choices create them.

Most leaders sit in the "decision zone"—waiting for more data, better timing, another opinion. They hesitate, hoping for clarity to arrive externally instead of creating it internally. But even those who do act often still operate as **decision-takers**, not **choice-makers**.

A decision is conditional—it reacts to circumstances.
And when things go wrong, decision-based leaders have an easy out:
"The market shifted." ... *"We didn't have the data."* ... *"Timing wasn't right."*

They were responsible for the decision—
but not truly **accountable for the outcome.**

A choice, on the other hand, is a commitment. It says:
"This is the direction. I'm owning it.
We're making it happen—no matter what."

That's the difference. Decisions look for the safest move.
Choices create the conditions for results—then take full ownership of making them real.

Great leaders operate in the "choice zone."
They create clarity, then take action—even with imperfect information.

They don't wait for certainty. They move with conviction.
That's what separates movement-makers from meeting-makers.

Your Job: Set the Intent, Step Out of the Way

Once you've set the destination and clarified what matters *now*, your next job is to **get the hell out of the way.**

Micromanagement is a symptom of unclear leadership. If you're constantly checking in, chasing people, and tweaking details—it usually means one of three things:

1. You didn't clarify the goal.
2. You don't trust the team to execute.
3. Or—more often—you don't trust **yourself** to let go.

Some leaders say they're empowering others, but they're addicted to chaos. They thrive on being the centre of the storm—issuing vague directions, keeping everyone guessing, staying indispensable.

That's not leadership.
That's a narcissistic control loop wrapped in a faux empowerment blanket. It creates confusion, dependency, and burnout.

Commander's Intent breaks this cycle..

It creates the guardrails, then hands over the wheel.

You'll still check progress.
You'll still course-correct.
But you won't need to babysit, and your team will feel more ownership—not less.

Case Study: Commander's Intent in Action

In 2003, during a major military operation in Iraq, a unit found itself cut off, behind enemy lines, with no communication.

No backup. No instructions. No command.

But they weren't paralysed—because they didn't need more instructions.

They had **Commander's Intent:**

> *"Secure the highway bridge by sunrise.*
> *Deny enemy control."*

Even though circumstances changed, the *intent* didn't. The team adapted their tactics, shifted roles, and got it done.

They didn't wait. They didn't freeze. They executed.

In business, the terrain shifts too—
just without bullets flying or the threat of capture and death.

A supplier folds. A key player quits. The market turns overnight.

In those moments, **clarity isn't optional—it's oxygen.**

If your team knows what matters, they can adjust.
If they don't, they stall.

The 5 Clarity Killers

Before we close this chapter, here are the biggest threats to clarity that cripple execution. Watch for these:

1. **Too Many Competing "Priorities":**
   If everything matters, nothing does.
   Set one priority at a time. Ruthlessly.

2. **Vague Language**
   "We're focusing on excellence"
   is neither clarity nor a real priority.
   Be specific. Use plain English. Set a target.

3. **Shifting Signals**
   If you change direction every week,
   your team stops trusting the map.
   Set the course. Stick to it.

4. **Fake Empowerment**
   Telling people to "take initiative"
   without clarity is a setup for failure.
   Empowerment without direction is abandonment.

5. **Clarity Hoarding**
   Keeping the real plan in your head while your team chases shadows wastes everyone's time. If you're clear, *share it.*
   Don't be the only one who knows what matters.

Clarity Audit: How Aligned Are You—Really?

Here's a quick self-check. Answer these honestly:

- If I asked your team right now, what's the single most important outcome this week—could they answer?
- Is your primary focus clear—and is it visible and understood by everyone?
- Are you reviewing it weekly—or just assuming people know?
- Do you talk in clarity or in slogans?

If any of those made you pause, good.
That's where your leadership work begins.

Chapter Recap: Lock This in

- Lack of clarity is a leadership failure, not a team flaw.
- Most teams are paralysed by conflicting demands disguised as priorities, vague goals, and shifting instructions.
- Commander's Intent is the clearest, most powerful model for creating autonomous execution.
- JFK's moon mission is the ultimate clarity move—short, bold, undeniable.
- You must learn to choose the path, not just "decide" when conditions are safe.
- Clarity removes friction, ignites momentum, and frees you from micromanagement.

What's Coming Next: The First Follower

Clarity is how you get attention. But clarity alone doesn't build movements. *People* do.

> In Chapter 2, you'll discover why the **most powerful leader** in any movement... isn't the person out front.

It's the first follower who says, "I believe in this," and brings others with them.

That's when your clarity turns into momentum.

Let's go there next.

Chapter Two

The First Follower Principle

Why Leadership is NOT About You

Leadership is not about being the star of the show.
It's about getting someone else to stand beside you—**first.**
And if you think this only applies to startups, you're wrong.

I've worked with businesses that have been operating for 10, 15, even 20 years, still being dragged forward by the founder.

No real believers.
No one who's truly bought in.
Just people doing what they're paid to do whilst the founder burns out trying to push it all uphill.

Same goes for enterprise businesses when a new division head steps into the role. They inherit the systems, the org chart, the budget—but if they don't earn their first true follower, someone who believes in their direction, they're just managing the status quo. Not leading.

The First Follower Principle applies whether you're launching or leading. Whether you're building something new or rebuilding something that's lost its way.

That first follower isn't just support—they're proof that your leadership works. And whether you realise it or not, that's the start of something bigger. **It's the start of creating a shift—creating movement.**

Most leaders don't think they're trying to create a movement. They're trying to lead a team, scale a business, or fix a mess.

But here's the truth:
When your message is clear—and one person believes in it deeply enough to act—**a movement has already started.**

Not the kind of movement that lands in headlines.
Not a cause. Not a campaign.

A *business movement* is something smaller, faster, and more powerful:

- It's when one person adopts the vision and takes action without waiting.
- When a shift in behaviour spreads—because someone believed, not because they were forced.
- When alignment becomes self-reinforcing, instead of top-down.

That's how execution scales.
Not through control, but through belief.
And that belief starts with a single person saying, *"I'm in."*

That's the real tipping point.
Movements don't start with vision. They start with *validation*.
Someone else stepping forward and saying, "I see it too."

This is the **First Follower Principle**—
and it's the moment when clarity turns into traction.

The Crazy Dance Guy (and the First Follower That Made Him a Leader)

If you've seen the famous *Crazy Dance Guy* video from a music festival, you already know how this works.

One guy is dancing like a maniac on a hill.
People laugh. Point. Watch.
But then—something critical happens:

Someone joins him.

Not because it's safe. Not because it's popular.
But because they *believe* in it—without needing more data, more confirmation, or a five-point strategic plan.

And that's when the shift happens.
Within seconds, a few more join in. Then dozens.
Then it's a full-on dance mob.

But the moment everything changed?
It wasn't when the first dancer started—it was when the first follower joined.

That's what turned a lone guy on a hill into a leader.
The First Follower transformed the act into a movement.

Why This Matters in Business

Most business leaders don't try to create something worth following. They spend their time trying to get people to follow **instructions**. Which is fine—if you want compliance.

But compliance isn't momentum.
It's not belief. And it's not leadership.
That kind of leadership is based on **imposed authority:**

"I pay you. I outrank you. So do what I say."

But the most powerful kind of authority isn't imposed—it's offered.

When someone chooses to follow you—before they have to, before it's safe—that's the moment your leadership becomes real. That's the moment your clarity starts to scale.

Because **First Followers aren't just doing what they're told.**
They're *buying in.*
And once someone buys in, they become a signal to everyone else:

"This is worth backing."

> **Side note:** In military leadership, authority is often seen as imposed—rank, command, protocol. But even in the military, the best leaders aren't followed just because of rank. They're followed because of clarity, consistency, and trust.

When we talk about "offered authority," we're talking about earned influence inside any system—whether that's a flat startup or a military unit.

You don't have to abandon structure to lead with belief.

What First Followers Actually Do:

- They give your vision *social proof.*
- They show others it's safe to follow.
- They often translate your clarity into action others can relate to.
- They create traction without bureaucracy.

First Followers aren't passive supporters—
they're the ones who **ignite action.**

If clarity is the spark, **First Followers are the ones who light the fuse.**

What Most Leaders Miss

Most leaders miss the moment.
Someone steps up. Takes initiative. Executes without being told.

But because the leader wasn't watching—or was too focused on their own spotlight—they ignore it. Or worse, criticise the method.

When you fail to recognise your First Follower, you don't just lose a moment—you lose momentum.

You lose loyalty. You lose trust. And eventually, you lose the kind of people who make your leadership matter.

First Followers are a gift. They believe before it's safe.
If you don't honour that belief, they won't stick around.
They'll find someone who sees them.

Real-World First Followers: The Hidden Force Behind Visionaries

Behind iconic leaders, there's almost always someone who **believed early**—and turned the vision into something others could follow.

These First Followers don't always get the spotlight, but without them, most "visionaries" would've stalled out at the start.

Let's look at a few that shaped entire industries:

Jobs had Wozniak

Steve Jobs had the vision, the pitch, the future-facing mindset.

But Steve Wozniak had the technical brilliance to build the first Apple computers with his own hands—on a shoestring.

He didn't wait for a funding round or a finished business plan.
He started building—*because he believed.*

That belief made Apple possible.
It gave the vision credibility before it had traction.

Musk had Gwynne Shotwell

Elon Musk is known for the audacity of his goals. But audacity alone doesn't launch rockets. Gwynne Shotwell brought rigour, operational brilliance, and engineering discipline to SpaceX.

She negotiated the contracts.
She built the systems.
She scaled the teams.

She turned Musk's "let's go to Mars" into actual aerospace credibility. Without her, SpaceX wouldn't have made it past PowerPoint.

Bezos had Jeff Wilke

Jeff Bezos saw the future of e-commerce.
But it was Jeff Wilke who made Amazon's operations world-class.

He was the architect of Amazon's supply chain engine—bringing structure, repeatability, and ruthless efficiency to an overwhelming vision.

While Bezos looked outward, Wilke built inward—turning potential into performance.

Walt had Roy Disney

Walt Disney dreamed big. Disneyland, Mickey, feature films.

But it was Roy Disney—his brother—who raised the money, balanced the budgets, and kept the business from falling apart.

Roy didn't just support the vision.
He funded it.
Protected it.
Delivered it.

Without Roy, Walt would've gone broke long before Mickey ever whistled.

In every one of these examples, the First Follower didn't just nod along They **believed before it was safe, acted without instruction**, and **amplified the vision with structure.**

They didn't replace the leader.
They made the leader's vision *real.*

What Attracts a First Follower

First Followers don't follow perfection.
They follow **conviction.**

They're not waiting for a detailed roadmap.
They're waiting for **clarity they can believe in,** and **a leader who actually stands for something.**

If your message is vague, if your energy is inconsistent, or if your vision shifts every week—don't expect anyone to follow early. They might follow eventually... but by then, it's no longer leadership. It's consensus.

The First Follower doesn't need more information.
*They need **something to believe in**—*
and someone who clearly believes it first.

First Followers Follow:

- ✓ **Conviction:**
  You don't need to be loud, but you do need to be certain.
- ✓ **Clarity:**
  If you can't explain it, they can't amplify it.
- ✓ **Consistency:**
  If your message changes every time you speak, they'll wait until you stabilise.
- ✓ **Ownership:**
  If you're not fully in, why should they be?

What They Don't Follow:

- ☒ "We're still figuring it out..."
- ☒ "Let's just try a few things and see what sticks..."
- ☒ "It's kind of like this... but also a bit like that..."
- ☒ "Just trust me." (without anything to actually trust)

First Followers don't follow slogans.
They follow *signals*—clarity, conviction, consistency.

You don't need to say "trust me" when you're already living in a way that earns it.

First Followers aren't needy.
They don't need your approval.
But they *do* need to see that you're willing to stake something on the vision—**your reputation, your energy, your belief.**

People don't follow clarity alone. They follow **the courage to stand in that clarity** before anyone else believes it.

Belief Without Execution Is Wasted

Clarity is the spark. The First Follower is the fuse.
But without **execution**, the whole thing fizzles out.
This is where most leaders fail.

They wait for more buy-in. More alignment. More readiness.
But momentum doesn't wait.

When your First Follower steps up, *that's your window.*
Miss it, and you may not get another one.

The Execution Window

There's a short moment after your First Follower commits—**before the crowd arrives**—when the energy is fragile but powerful.

This is the ignition zone.
If you feed it, momentum builds.
If you hesitate, it dies.

Execution isn't just about doing.
It's about doing while the belief is fresh.

That moment when your First Follower steps in?
Don't ignore it.
Don't downplay it.

Acknowledge it. Amplify it. Validate it.

In that Crazy Dance Guy video, the leader doesn't just keep dancing.

He turns and celebrates the person who joined him.
He says—in body language—"*You matter.*"

That simple act is what opens the floodgates.
It tells everyone watching:

"This isn't just about me. It's about us."

Without that moment of validation, the dance would've stayed a solo.

The Role of the Leader at This Stage

Once the First Follower moves, your job isn't to micromanage—it's to amplify.

- Make the vision visible.
- Remove friction.
- Support the belief with resources, trust, and space.
- Show the rest of the team that this isn't a "test"—this *is* the direction.

Belief becomes contagious *only when backed by motion.*

What Happens If You Miss It?

- **Early believers disengage.**
- **The team watches—and does nothing.**
- **The window closes.**
  And just like that, you're back to pushing instead of leading.

Business Reality Check

In business, the First Follower might not be a dramatic moment.
They might not be dancing on a hill or launching a rocket.

They might just be the first person on your team who says,
"I've got this," and starts moving—
before you've built the deck or booked the meeting.

That moment is easy to miss.
But if you're paying attention, it's your biggest asset.
Because in business, **momentum doesn't start with a big speech.**
It starts when one person takes aligned action—
and others see it.

This is the handoff point from belief to momentum.
From clarity to movement.
From intention to execution.

And that's where we go next.

> **In Chapter 3,** we'll break down how to build momentum through **clarity in action**—and why the fewer steps you give your team, the faster they move.

Chapter Three

The Execution Equation

Why Less = More Action

The Myth of More

Activity Isn't Execution

Most teams look busy. They're flooded with meetings, messages, decks, dashboards, and Slack threads. **But activity isn't execution.** It's often just inertia dressed up as momentum.

The brutal truth?
Most teams are over-informed and under-executing.

They don't need more strategy. They don't need more resources.
They need clarity, fewer decisions, faster action,
and permission to move.

Execution isn't about having all the answers.
It's about having the freedom to act on the ones you already have.

Execution Equation:

Fewer decisions + more ownership = faster outcomes

This isn't theory!
It's the pattern you see in every high-output team—from elite military units to high-growth companies.

Fewer decisions.
More autonomy.
Faster momentum.

Why Most Leaders Get This Wrong

Leaders try to "support" their team by:

- Keeping them in every loop.
- Asking for constant updates.
- Giving input on every step.
- Holding alignment meetings to clarify what should already be clear.

The result?
Indecision by overload.

The more layers you add, the slower things get.
The more decisions you centralise, the more bottlenecks you create.

So how do you get it right?

Do the opposite—deliberately.

- Keep people focused on one outcome, not a dozen competing demands.
- Reduce how often they need your approval.
- Clarify what done looks like, so they can move without circling back.

The best leaders don't manage every move.
They remove the friction—and get out of the way.

The Real Role of a 20% Leader

You're not there to run everything.
You're there to make execution *easier to start* and *harder to stall.*

That means:

- Cut the steps.
- Simplify the decision.
- Make the goal clear enough that your team can act without asking.

If your team is asking for permission, you haven't given them clarity.
If they're waiting, you haven't removed the friction.

Execution isn't about pressure.
It's about *removing resistance.*

Real-World Case: Netflix vs Blockbuster

Execution failure doesn't always look like chaos.
Sometimes it looks like *waiting for approval* while someone else moves.

Blockbuster had the resources. The data. The brand.
But their decision-making was slow, centralised, and risk-averse. Every new idea had to fight its way through layers of permission and politics.

Meanwhile, Netflix operated lean. They empowered small teams, removed red tape, and made bold decisions fast—with full ownership.

Blockbuster delayed. Netflix executed. One is now a business school case study. The other is your streaming login.

If you want to go fast, go alone. If you want to go far, go together.
If you want to go fast and far, give your team permission to move.

The F.A.S.T. Execution Model

Execution accelerates when clarity meets trust.
The best teams move with speed—not because they're reckless, but because their leaders remove friction and protect focus. **That's what F.A.S.T. execution looks like:**

Focus on the outcome
Autonomy to act
Speed over polish
Trust in each other

This is how you build velocity *without chaos.*
Not with more meetings—but with fewer roadblocks.

The Hollywood Execution Model

Why movies get made while your projects stall

What Business Can Learn from a Movie Set

While I've had experience in film finance, let me be clear: I'm not in the movie business, and no, I'm not looking for film scripts or projects to fund.

Film finance is one of the most over-hyped, underperforming arenas for capital—and most private investors are approached only after every other avenue has failed.

You're the last resort, not the first pick.
And once you're in, you have zero real influence.

But through that exposure, I learned something valuable—especially from conversations with my friend **Jennifer Fiedler**, a seasoned Hollywood film producer who's now a respected leadership coach.

Jennifer's insights into how films actually get made (or don't) gave me a real window into *execution under fire*—where deadlines are non-negotiable, pressure is constant, and the team only works because everyone knows exactly what they're doing.

In the film world execution isn't a talking point.
It's the difference between a finished product and a financial disaster.

Through my conversations with Jennifer—some personal, some collaborative—I learned that the execution discipline behind film production is on another level.

In film, things *must* get done—on time, on budget, no matter what. The margins are brutal. There's no safety net, and it all happens with an execution standard most businesses would crumble under.

What follows is a view into how execution works in Hollywood—and what business can learn from it.

Urgency Without Excuses

In Hollywood, deadlines aren't optional.
You shoot today—or you miss the shot.
Simple.

You don't hear
"Let's push the scene until next week" ... or...
"We're still workshopping the script."

The location is booked.
The permits are active.
The crew is on the clock.
The actors and extras are in place.

It has to happen—because not doing it isn't an option.

So it does.

Brutal Clarity, Real Deadlines

Every person on a set knows their role.
They're not wondering what's important.
They're not checking in five times a day or looking for last-minute clarification.

They know exactly what's expected of them, and they deliver—and if they don't deliver, they're replaced. ***Swiftly.***

This isn't cruelty. This isn't chaos. **It's clarity at scale.**

> *In the film world, it's simple:*
> ***Do your job, or someone else will ... Today***

It's not brutality. It's efficiency.
It's high-stakes, high-speed, high-performance, and it works—because **everyone knows the mission, the moment, and the margin for error.**

The Right People in the Right Roles

Everyone on that set was chosen for one reason:

They're the best person for that specific job.

They're not learning on the fly.
They've done it before, and they're trusted to do it again—fast.

If someone fails to deliver, they're replaced.
No drama. No three-month transition.

Just the next expert stepping in immediately—ready to go.

They're on set the same day or next day depending on travel requirements.

It's not about being ruthless.
It's about being ready.

Execution isn't personal. It's operational.

This kind of execution discipline might sound cold or transactional—but it's not. The film industry runs on people doing what they love, what they're exceptional at, and what they've trained for.

It's not about control. It's about clarity.
The right person, in the right role, aligned to the right outcome.
And when that alignment breaks, they don't coddle—they correct. Fast.

Built for Speed, Not Safety Nets

Producers don't run 3-month hiring processes.
Jennifer once told me that serious producers always have a backup.

They know who they'll call next if someone fails to deliver.
They're not scrambling—they're *prepared.*

It's not about job security. It's about mission security.
If someone drops the ball, someone else steps in.

If a key crew member doesn't show up, someone's already been briefed.
If the sound tech fails, they've got another ready to fly in.
Not hypothetically. Literally.

In business, this sounds harsh.
In film, it's standard.

No bloated org charts. No "alignment meetings". No reporting cycles. Just execution. Scene by scene. Day by day.

That's not paranoia.
That's execution infrastructure.
It's a mindset business should adopt—not the showbiz, but the systems.

What Business Can Learn from Hollywood

- ✓ **Set real deadlines—and keep them.**
- ✓ **Define every role before the project starts.**
- ✓ **Expect delivery—and have a backup plan ready.**
- ✓ **Build a network, not dependencies.**
- ✓ **Get it done, or get replaced.**
- ✓ **Hire for delivery—not potential.**

In a film crew, no one says, "I didn't know we were rolling today"—unless they spent the night doing lines of cocaine and bathing in bourbon at the local strip club ... in which case ... Exit stage right.

That's the mindset business needs to borrow—
not the glamour, not the script, but the grit and the shot list.
Stay on task or don't let the door hit your arse on the way out.

The Execution Mindset

How to create a culture of fast movement without chaos

It's Not About Speed. It's About Elimination.

Execution isn't about moving fast.
It's about removing everything that slows you down.

Most leaders don't have an execution problem.
They have a friction problem—and they tolerate it.

They tolerate slow approvals.
They tolerate bloated systems.
They tolerate meetings that solve nothing, documents no one reads, and roles no one owns.

The team isn't underperforming.
The environment is overcomplicated.

Simplify or Stall

Fast cultures aren't chaotic. They're just **clean.**
Fewer steps.
Fewer layers.
Fewer excuses.

Execution doesn't come from motivational posters or team huddles.
It comes from **brutal clarity, real ownership, and no escape routes.**

The minute someone says,
"I didn't know I could make that call"—
you've failed.

If your team is stuck, it's not because they're slow.
It's because ***you've made it hard to move.***

The Leader's Mirror: 5 Hard Questions

If execution is stalling, stop looking at your team.
Start looking in the mirror.
Ask yourself:

1. **Where am I tolerating delay disguised as planning?**
2. **What decisions am I clinging to that should be delegated?**
3. **What bottlenecks exist because I haven't been clear?**
4. **Where have I created complexity that protects me from being wrong?**
5. **Who's waiting for me to lead—but I'm too busy pretending I already did?**

If you feel a little sick reading those, good.
That's where the reset begins.

Execution Is a Culture. You Build It or You Kill It.

Execution isn't a "phase."
It's a leadership choice—repeated daily.

You either build a culture that moves, or one that waits.
You either build a team that acts, or one that checks in.
There's no neutral.

> **In Chapter 4,** we get ruthless.
> We cut, we simplify, we strip out the dead weight.
> Because **once you're moving, focus is everything.**

Chapter Four

Cut Faster, Move Smarter

Deletion is a leadership skill

Kill the Noise

You Don't Need More Time—You Need Less Noise

Most teams aren't struggling from lack of effort.
They're drowning in inputs.

Meetings, Slack threads, dashboards, project updates, "quick syncs," task lists, follow-ups, reports...

Everyone's busy.
No one's clear.

They're reacting to everything—without driving anything.

The Illusion of Productivity

Busy feels good. It feels productive.
You tick off tasks. You sit through meetings.
You reply fast. You stay "across it."
But here's the truth:

Activity ≠ Execution.
Responsiveness ≠ Leadership.
Noise ≠ Movement.

If your calendar is full but your priorities are foggy, you're not winning—you're leaking energy.

Deletion Is a Leadership Skill

Great leaders don't just focus—they remove.

They delete:

- ☒ Meetings that don't move outcomes.
- ☒ Reports no one reads.
- ☒ Updates that add noise, not value.
- ☒ Metrics that don't lead to better decisions.

They cut fast and without guilt.

What you remove is just as important as what you initiate. Every unnecessary input is friction against execution.

On Purpose vs Busy By Default

Most teams aren't working on purpose.

They're working **by default**—chained to habits that no longer serve them.

Your job isn't to get them to do more.
Your job is to make sure **every action is on purpose.**

Real-World Case: Dropbox's $1.2 Billion Focus Decision

In 2013, Dropbox was managing dozens of side projects—photo apps, email experiments, even a new kind of collaborative doc platform.

The team was stretched. Progress stalled. Execution slowed to a crawl.

So the founders made a brutal decision:
They cut almost everything.

They shut down Mailbox.
Sunsetted Carousel.
Scrapped half the roadmap.

All to focus on one thing: *the core file-sync product.*

Investors thought they were crazy.

Then usage spiked. Retention grew. Revenue exploded.

Within 18 months, they added $1.2 billion in valuation.

Focus wasn't the cost—it was the unlock.
They didn't scale by adding more. They scaled by deleting the drag.

> *"A great strategy isn't what you add. It's what you're willing to eliminate."*
>
> *—Greg McKeown, Essentialism*

Simplify to Scale

Complexity is a handbrake, not a badge of honour

Complexity Creeps. Simplicity Scales.

No business sets out to be complex.
But complexity shows up in layers:

- Another tool.
- Another approval.
- Another "quick process".
- Another department workaround.

Suddenly you've got fifteen dashboards and no clarity.

Complexity Feels Smart. But It's Slowing You Down.

Complex systems feel sophisticated.
They look like you're running a grown-up operation.

But the truth is this:

> **If your team can't explain what matters in one breath, you're scaling confusion.**
> Complexity creates drag.
> Simplicity creates flow.

What Simplicity Actually Looks Like

Simplicity doesn't mean shallow. It means:

- ✓ Every system has a reason.
- ✓ Every step drives an outcome.
- ✓ Every person knows how they contribute.
- ✓ Every team has fewer options, but clearer ones.

The result?
Speed, alignment, and reduced friction.

Real-World Case: Apple's 100 No's

When Steve Jobs returned to Apple in 1997, the company had over 300 active products. No one knew what to focus on. The brand was tanking. Execution was scattered.

Jobs famously slashed the roadmap to just four quadrants:
Consumer vs pro,
Desktop vs portable.
Everything else got killed.

The company nearly died. Then it roared back.

> *"I'm actually as proud of the things we haven't done as the things I have done,"* Jobs said.
> ***"Innovation is saying no to 1,000 things."***

That's not a mindset. That's a system.

Simplification Filters You Can Steal

Want to simplify? Start asking:

- Is this driving the outcome—or just tracking it?
- Would we design it this way if we started today?
- What happens if we just don't do this?

You don't need 50 filters. You need one question on repeat:

What's the fastest path to the outcome—and what's in the way?

Your Focus Ritual

Build the clarity habit that keeps execution sharp

Clarity Isn't a One-Time Thing

You don't "set clarity" once and expect it to last. It erodes—daily. It gets buried in inboxes, Slack threads, tasks, and meetings.

If you don't protect clarity, chaos will replace it.

The best leaders don't have more hours.
They have **fewer distractions** and **stronger resets**.

The Competitive Advantage No One Talks About

Here's what no one admits in boardrooms—but top performers rely on:

Meditation.

Not incense. Not loud chanting.
Just space to *stop reacting and reset intention.*

We recommend **Transcendental Meditation (TM)**—two 20-minute sessions a day. But even one focused 10-minute pause can change the shape of your day.

More than simply "clearing your mind", TM
or meditation in general is about sharpening it—
so you stop confusing noise with signal.

A clear mind doesn't need more time.
It just makes faster decisions.

The 3-Step Focus Reset

Use this simple ritual weekly—or whenever you feel the clutter building:

1. **Delete one obligation**
   A meeting, a report, a task—something that adds drag.
2. **Clarify the one priority**
   What outcome matters this week above all else?
3. **Schedule one window**
   20 minutes, no phone, no meetings. Just thinking space.

Repeat as needed. Scale it across your leadership team.

Daily, Weekly, and Quarterly Focus Habits

Daily

- Start the day with a handwritten focus point.
- Block one 20-minute "deep clarity" window (even if it's in the car).

Weekly

- End Friday by asking: *What can we stop doing next week?*
- Start Monday by stating: *What matters most now?*

Quarterly

- Review your team's signal-to-noise ratio.
- Delete dead projects, unclear goals, redundant processes.

You don't build execution through pressure.
You build it through clarity—
and protect it like your business depends on it.

Because it does.

Clarity gets you moving.
Focus keeps you aligned.
Energy is what sustains the execution.

If you want to go the distance (and take your team with you) you need more than goals and systems.
You need **fuel**.

> That's what **Chapter 5** is about.
> How to **lead with energy that doesn't burn out.**
> How to build momentum that isn't forced.
> How to create a culture that runs on **pleasure, passion, and purpose**—not pressure.

You've simplified the system. Now we wire it for energy.

Chapter Five

Leading With Fire

Why joy isn't a luxury, it's a weapon

Pleasure Drives Performance

If It Feels Good, You're Doing It Right

Most leaders have been conditioned to believe that if they're not grinding, they're not growing. If it feels good, it must be a distraction.

That's backwards.

Pleasure isn't the enemy of performance. It's the fuel.

When you enjoy what you're doing—
even in sprints, even under pressure—
you execute faster, recover quicker, and stay in the game longer.

The Neurochemistry of Flow

Here's the science:

- **Dopamine** = the chemical of motivation and momentum.
- **Pleasure** increases dopamine.
- **Dopamine** increases focus, learning speed, decision-making, and execution.

It's not a motivational poster. It's brain chemistry.

If your team isn't feeling small wins, progress, or enjoyment, they're not just bored. They're chemically starved for performance.

The "Grind" is Not the Goal

You weren't put on this planet to suffer through meetings and force yourself to execute through exhaustion.
Neither was your team.

You were built to move with energy—fueled by challenge, reward, meaning, and *moments of joy.*

High performers don't run on pressure.
They run on **purposeful progress that feels good.**

If execution feels like a punishment, it's not sustainable.
If it feels like progress, momentum builds itself.

What Pleasure Looks Like in Practice

This isn't about ping pong tables, cupcakes or open beer taps.

It's about:

- ✓ Making fast decisions and feeling momentum hit.
- ✓ Winning together in short sprints.
- ✓ Seeing clear progress.
- ✓ Doing work that feels *just hard enough to stretch, but not break.*

Smart leaders engineer pleasure into performance—on purpose.

Micro-Pleasure: The Execution Multiplier

Inject micro-pleasure into your team rhythm:

- ▹ Start a meeting with "what's working".
- ▹ Let someone ship something early and own the win.
- ▹ Recognise visible momentum in the moment.
- ▹ Cut the junk that drags morale down, even if it looks "productive" on paper.

Every time your team feels progress they lean in harder.

Here's the hard data:

- A 2024 report from **Time Doctor** found that **82% of employees** cite happiness and engagement as key productivity drivers.
- **A University of Warwick** study (cited by Forbes in 2024) showed that happy workers are **12% more productive.**
- And according to **Oxford University**, that figure climbs to **13%** in environments that promote day-to-day enjoyment.

This isn't about perks—it's about performance states.

Need proof?

At **IDEO**, one of the world's most respected design firms, teams are empowered to shape how they work—not just what they deliver.

It's not about comfort.
It's about *creative satisfaction.*

The result?
High output, fast cycles, low churn.

Pleasure isn't a distraction. It's a multiplier.
Smart leaders engineer it on purpose.

Passion Fuels Ownership

When people care, you don't need to chase them

Motivation Is Cheap. Passion Moves Mountains.

Most teams are motivated.
Motivated to keep their job.
Motivated to hit a KPI.
Motivated to not get in trouble.

That's not passion.
That's survival.

Passion is what happens when someone stops renting their role and starts owning it.

When someone believes in the mission—when they care about the outcome—you don't have to chase them.
You don't have to manage every step.

They self-correct.
They overdeliver.
They *lead*.

Passion Creates Internal Pressure

You can't force it. But you can *unleash* it.

People want to care. They want to feel like their work matters, that it connects to something real.

When that happens?
Execution doesn't need enforcement. It becomes instinct.

Passion turns direction into drive.
It's what gets people to say, "I've got this", without being told.

The Risk: Passion Without Clarity = Burnout

Here's the trap:
Leaders love passion—
but if you don't match it with focus, you get burnout fast.

Passionate people will run through walls. But if you don't show them which wall matters, they'll exhaust themselves breaking the wrong one.

Don't waste your best people's energy on unclear goals.

Passion needs constraints. It thrives in direction.
But direction isn't just an individual concept—it becomes cultural.

If no one resets the tone, your team builds a default setting—a kind of emotional autopilot. And over time, that autopilot becomes the atmosphere your team breathes, especially under pressure.

Set the Tone. Don't Let It Set You.

Your team has a frequency too. It's not written in values posters or strategy decks—it's what shows up under pressure.

That *default tone*? That's your **organisational setpoint.**

Some teams default to urgency. Others to creativity.
Some hit chaos, retreat into blame, or just float in passive apathy.

Setpoints aren't built in crisis—they're revealed by it.
And if you don't consciously reset them, they run the show.

High-performance teams don't just optimise for clarity or systems.
They engineer a baseline energy that makes forward motion feel normal.

Want to shift it? *You don't need a keynote or a rebrand.*

Just start with questions like:

- What tone do we return to under stress or silence?
- Are updates energising—or exhausting?
- Are we celebrating progress—or just surviving the week?

Resetting your setpoint can be as simple as asking what's working in a planning session—or killing the dead projects no one believes in but everyone drags forward.

When you change the emotional baseline, execution follows.

See the **Organisation Setpoints** breakdown in the **Energy Toolkit** at the back of the book.

Passion = Belief + Autonomy

Want passion? Build it.

- **Give people something to believe in:**
  Be explicit about what matters.
  Share the why behind the work.
  Show them who benefits and how.

- **Give them the space to own how they get there:**
  Set the outcome.
  Let them design the path.
  Skip the micromanagement.
  Ask for *directional updates*, not daily status reports.

- **Remove the friction that kills momentum:**
  Kill redundant approvals.
  Streamline tools.
  Give clear constraints and decision rights.

- **Protect them from chaos and noise:**
  Don't change priorities weekly.
  Don't overload the roadmap.
  Guard their focus like it's your own.

Passion grows in the soil of belief.
But it only survives when it has room to move.

Real-World Micro-Case: Early SpaceX Teams

Early SpaceX engineers weren't working for big pay.
They weren't chasing titles.
They were **obsessed** with making private space flight real.

They worked 100-hour weeks.
Slept in offices. Blew past every limit.
Not because someone forced them—
but because they *cared more than anyone else.*

That's passion. And it wasn't managed.
It was *protected*—by clarity of mission and removal of distractions.

You're the Limit Until You're the Lift

If you want to build passionate teams that push through friction and lead without handholding, you need more than incentives or vision statements. You need leaders operating from the right *frequency*.

That's why we use the **Frequency Ladder for Leaders**—adapted from the work of **Dr. David R. Hawkins**, author of *Power vs. Force.*

Hawkins proposed that every emotional state carries a measurable frequency. Whether or not you buy the numbers, the patterns hold.

You can see it play out daily in leadership behaviour.

Most people leading companies don't operate at high frequencies.
They live between **grief, fear, desire, anger, and pride.**
They'll spike into courage when forced.

Occasionally, they'll wick up into reason or clarity—
but like an overbought stock chart, they retrace.
They don't hold the level.
They haven't trained the muscle to stay there.

I've seen this pattern for over 30 years—across founders, CEOs, and senior executives. Many of them weren't weak. They weren't even struggling by conventional standards.

But they were stuck—
looping through the same low-frequency patterns, sometimes for years.

They'd operate from fear, spike into anger,
retreat into pride, then collapse into grief.
Some would bounce up briefly into courage or clarity, but rarely hold it.

They built companies.
They drove results.

But they also created collateral damage—
burnt-out staff, missed opportunities, cultures of silence. And because they were moving fast and hitting goals, no one challenged them.

The team just kept quiet.
The dysfunction was invisible to the person causing it.

Some bounce.
Some burn out.
But many just *loop*—successfully.

They run fast on the hamster wheel of pressure, pride, and short-term intensity.

They still build.
They still win.
But they do it with high collateral damage—burned-out teams, missed leverage, and a ceiling they'll never see until it hits them in the face.

Their team sees it long before they do. But no one speaks up.

Because when the one leading the company operates in force—not frequency—silence feels safer than truth.

That's what this Ladder is about.

It's not a personality test.
It's a mirror.

It's not about perfection.
It's about pattern.

Where are you consistently leading from—
and what is that costing or compounding inside your team?

Full breakdown in the **Energy Toolkit** at the end of this book.

But here's the takeaway:
If you want execution that accelerates, you need leadership that vibrates above the noise.

Your team won't rise above your frequency.
Make sure you're setting the bar where it belongs.

Shift State. Lead Better.

You can't lead from tension and expect traction.
If your energy is off, your execution will be too.

Smart leaders don't wait for clarity—they trigger it.
They use simple tools to shift state fast and take control of the tone.

We break them down in the **Energy Toolkit** at the back of this book.
Start with:

- **The 17-Second Reset:**
  Shift your frequency in 17 seconds—then build unstoppable momentum in under 68.
- **Clarity Anchors:**
  Snap back to high ground with a cue that pulls you out of chaos and into control.
- **Leader Signal Checks:**
  Your energy is louder than your words. Know what you're broadcasting—before it backfires.
- **Momentum Cues:**
  Plug energy leaks and inject drive into your team—in 60 seconds or less.

They're fast.
They work.
And they're built for pressure, not retreats.

Lead from a better state—on purpose.

Purpose Creates Resilience

When the mission matters, people push through

Clarity gets you moving

Purpose is your pressure shield.
Every business hits walls.
Deadlines get missed. Markets shift. Teams get tired.

What keeps them going isn't process.
It's **belief**—that what they're building matters beyond the spreadsheet.

Purpose keeps you standing when the plan blows up.

The Science of Meaning and Performance

High-pressure jobs don't break people. **Pointless jobs do.**

When people can see how their work connects to a bigger mission, they:

- Push longer without burning out.
- Bounce back faster after setbacks.
- Make better decisions under stress.
- Take greater ownership—even when no one's watching.

It's not fluffy. It's psychological endurance.

When people believe in the mission, they stop looking for exits.

Make Purpose Operate, Not Sit on the Wall

Too many companies treat purpose like a marketing tagline or a leadership offsite exercise.

Our purpose should do something real:
Help you make better decisions, faster.
Ask:

- Does this project serve the mission?
- Will this move us toward the impact we want to make?
- If we win here, *who else wins?*

Purpose clarifies what matters when everything feels urgent.

How to Reinforce Purpose (Without Turning Into a TED Talk)

Want to keep purpose alive? Here's how to do it without preaching:

- **Tell real stories** about who you're helping and why it matters.
- **Connect outcomes to humans**, not just metrics.
- **Repeat the "why" behind the work** until your team can repeat it without you.
- **Kill the work that doesn't serve the mission—** visibly and decisively.
- **Use purpose as a heat map:** if people are disengaging, purpose is fading.

You don't need a town hall.
You need truth, repetition, and ruthless alignment.

Real-World Case: Patagonia's Purpose in Action

When Patagonia ran a full-page ad saying *"Don't Buy This Jacket"*, it wasn't a gimmick.

It was a reflection of their purpose:
environmental stewardship, not endless consumption.

It resonated because it was real.
They didn't just say it—they *operated* on it.

Their purpose shaped hiring, product design, marketing, and even their Black Friday strategy.

Result? One of the most loyal customer bases and highest employee retention rates in retail.

Purpose isn't what you say.
It's what you protect, especially when it costs you something.

When pressure hits, your systems will wobble.
But if the *purpose* is strong, the people will hold.

You've got the frameworks.
You've got the fire.
Now it's time to do something with it.

The next 30 days can reset how you lead, how your team moves, and how fast you get results.

Not by adding more.
By executing better—*on purpose.*

Chapter 6 is your blueprint.
If you choose to use it, you'll **build your execution muscle** one sharp move at a time.

Chapter Six

The 30-Day Reset Challenge

Rewire your execution in 30 days—20% at a time

This is a tactical system reboot. A sharp, 30-day sprint to delete the drag, rebuild clarity, and relight the fire—without adding complexity. If your team's moving, but not accelerating, this is where you fix it.

The Why Behind the Challenge

You don't need more time—you need a reset

Execution Evolution is a Myth. Execution Degrades!

Left alone, execution doesn't get smarter.
It gets slower.

Heavier. Clumsier. Messier.
More layers. More drag. Less movement.
Bloated with good intentions and bad processes.

That's not a strategy problem.
That's a *leadership operating system failure.*

Most teams don't stall because they're broken. They stall because they never stop to cut, refocus, and hit reset.

Execution degrades unless you intervene—surgically.
And no—this isn't micromanagement.
You're not jumping in to rescue.

You're stepping in to recalibrate—fast and clean.
Trim the sail. Don't grab the oars.

Great leaders don't course-correct because their team is weak.
They do it to keep speed, alignment, and pressure locked in tight.
This challenge fixes that.

You Can't Optimise What's Clogged

Your calendar is full. Your systems are stacked. Your people are tired.

So what do most leaders do? They throw in more:

- Another dashboard.
- Another sync.
- Another tool.
- Another "quick fix" meeting.

That's not execution.
That's noise with branding.

So don't patch over the pressure
Start clearing the pipe.

This reset works because it strips back everything that's bloated, misaligned, or just plain useless.

- One outcome per week.
- One move per day.
- One layer of friction cut at a time.

Simple structure.
Sharp cuts.
Fast relief.
That's how you make execution breathe again.

Reboot Execution. Cut Before it Collapses.

Weak leaders coast through slowdowns,
hoping things will fix themselves.

The great ones don't wait for the stall.
They see it coming—and move early.
They treat execution like a trader reads the market:

Spot the dip. Read the retrace.
Step in before the stall becomes a spiral.

Smart leaders act before execution hits the wall—
not when it's already broken.

Think of it like trading:
You don't wait for a crash—you read the signal before the slide.

The reset is preventative precision avoiding the need to react, scramble and possibly end up catching a falling knife.

The 30-Day Reset is built for that kind of move.
It's built to stop a disaster from happening,
instead of trying to fix it post-mortem.

To help you lead cleaner, sharper, and harder—
without burning out your team or yourself.

- ✓ Strip out dead weight.
- ✓ Re-activate the 20% of actions that move 80% of results.
- ✓ Lock in rituals that create clarity, speed, and ownership.

Not theory.
Just one move a day.
Done with intent.
Backed by systems that stick.

Let's be honest, most leaders never pause long enough to reset the system. They just push harder until the whole damned thing groans.

This challenge forces the pause—
and directs it with purpose.

This Challenge Is Built for:

- Leaders running too hot for too long.
- Teams who've lost their edge but still have fire.
- Or anyone who's hit that point where everything's technically "fine"—but nothing's *really* moving.

If you're reading this, you don't need more ideas.
You need movement.

Want Something Smaller First?

This is the 30-day reset. It's tactical, sharp, and self-paced.

But if you want a faster ignition point—something that gets the engine firing without committing to a full cycle—we've also built a **Serial Spark Sequence.**

It's a 5-day strike built to hit one execution bottleneck, fast.

One friction point.
Five laser-focused days to fix it.
Clean execution. Zero fluff. Quick combustion.

You can run it solo or with your team. And if you want backup? Reach out. Capacity for one-on-one support is limited—and if we can help immediately, we will. If not, we'll line up a time that works.

No pitch. No funnel.
Just help. One-on-one.

The 30-Day Playbook

4 Weeks. 4 Focus Shifts. 1 Execution Reset.

What This Is and How It Works

The 30-Day Reset sharpens execution by cutting through clutter, drag, and decision fatigue.

Each week targets a different layer.
Each day delivers one deliberate, high-impact move.

You won't need to guess if it's working.
Your team will feel the difference—
faster decisions, clearer direction, fewer stalls.

Energy shifts. Friction drops.
And the better you lead it, the faster they respond.

This is your reset.
But **they're the proof it's working.**

Week 1: Clarity + Deletion

Cut the noise.
Strip the drag.
Find what actually moves the needle.

Before you add speed, strip the drag. This week is about focus—cutting the noise, surfacing what actually matters, and deleting dead weight fast.

Day 1: Kill One Recurring Meeting That Adds No Value

Look at your calendar with brutal honesty. Pick one recurring meeting that burns time without driving outcomes—and kill it.

Don't reschedule it.
Don't reframe it.
Delete it.
Let your team know you're doing it to protect their time, not just yours.

This one cut instantly restores space and sends a signal: clarity is more important than routine.

Day 2: Define "What Winning Looks Like" This Week

Most teams don't slow down because they're unmotivated—they slow down because they're unclear. Motivation follows clarity.

Write one sentence that defines success this week.
Not three bullet points.
Not a waffle-filled strategy deck.

One clear sentence: *"By Friday, we will have ______."*
Share it. Anchor everything else to it.

Day 3: Delete One System, Tool, or Process You Don't Actually Need

Every business accumulates clutter. A dashboard no one reads. A tool nobody uses. A process that made sense six months ago—but now just burns time.

Pick one.Remove it.
Watch what breaks.
If nothing breaks, it didn't matter.

Day 4: Ask Your Team What's Slowing Them Down—Then Cut It

Don't guess.

Ask:
"What's one thing slowing you down this week?"

It might be a process, a person, a platform, or a permission circuit.
Take action on one of their answers.
Fast.

Don't promise a restructure—just make a clean cut they can feel.

Day 5: Identify Your 20% Action

What's the one thing you personally do that moves 80% of your results?

Not what's important.
What creates movement.
Identify it. Name it.

That's your 20% **action**—protect it ruthlessly for the rest of the challenge.

Week 2: Ownership + Focus

Fewer bottlenecks.
Clearer lanes.
Stronger accountability.

Clear lanes, sharper roles, faster movement.
This week builds accountability by shifting decision-making out of bottlenecks and back into the hands of your team.

Day 6: Define One Decision Your Team Should Own—Then Hand It Over

You're the leader, not the gatekeeper.

Choose one decision that your team has been waiting on you for—then stop being the bottleneck.

Give them the guardrails, the mission, and the autonomy to own it.
Let go, loudly and clearly.

Day 7: Create a Personal Not-To-Do List

You've got a to-do list.
Now make a not-to-do list.

Write down three tasks, habits, or distractions you'll stop doing this week because they don't serve your 20% focus.

Visibility creates discipline.
Simplicity creates traction.

Day 8: Ask Your Team What They're Waiting on You For—Then Cut the Chain

Ask your team:
"What are you waiting on me for that you shouldn't be?"

Don't defend.
Don't explain.
Just listen—and find one chain you can cut.

Ownership thrives when you remove the dependency culture.

Day 9: Eliminate One Approval Circuit

Pick one approval circuit that's slowing people down and eliminate it.

If someone needs to get sign-off to move forward on something that's under their remit, **that's not ownership—it's permission addiction.**

Cut it, and trust them to move.

Day 10: Find Your First Follower—and Give Them More Rope

You know who they are—
the one who gets it without overthinking it.
The one who steps up without being asked.

That's your first follower.
Now stretch their lane.

Give them one task, project, or decision to fully own—
without needing to loop you in.

Week 3: Momentum + Movement

Speed without scramble.
Progress without burnout.

This is where you shift from effort to flow.

Remove blockers, amplify wins, and install progress signals that create self-sustaining motion.

Day 11: Complete One Open Circuit

That half-finished thing on your to-do list?
Close it.

Every unfinished task creates drag.
Pick one project, promise, or process that's hanging—
and either finish it or kill it.

Completion creates relief.
Relief creates motion.

Day 12: Celebrate One Visible Win—With Impact

Find one piece of progress your team has made—
and highlight the *impact*, not just the effort.

Call out what changed, what outcome it created, and why it mattered to the client or business.

That's how momentum spreads.

Day 13: Ask What Increasing Momentum Would Look Like

Ask your team:
"What would it look like if we increased momentum?"

Would we move faster?
Or would we add more weight to what matters?

Their answers show you what's dragging—
and what's worth accelerating.

Day 14: Remove One Blocker

Blockers aren't always big.

Sometimes they're clunky tools, outdated handoffs, approval chains, or unclear ownership.

Find one. Cut it clean.
Let the team feel the release.

Day 15: Set a Signal That You're Moving

Choose one simple signal that shows you're moving in the right direction.

Not a KPI (not least of all because KPI's are productivity and performance killers. *Why? Ask me.*).
Not a dashboard filler. A signal.

It might be a client decision made, a roadblock removed, or a critical handoff completed.

Make it real.
Make it visible. Make it matter.

Week 4: Energy + Endurance

Keep the engine clean.
Protect your clarity.
Build a system that holds under pressure.

Time to protect the engine.
This week sharpens habits, cuts energy leaks, and puts joy and strategic space back into your system.

Day 16: Audit Your Calendar for Energy Leaks

Your calendar is a statement of your leadership focus.
Stop treating it like a schedule. Start treating it like a scoreboard.

Look back over the last two weeks—what drained you?
What felt like work without outcome?

Cut one.
Reframe one (change its intent or who runs it).
Batch the rest—cluster shallow tasks and free up space for thinking.

Day 17: Block Strategic Focus Time—Then Guard It

Book a 90-minute deep-focus block.
Not for catching up. Not for admin. For *thinking*.
Name the block, protect the time,
and use it to solve a real problem that matters.

This is leadership time.
The part where you stop reacting and start directing.

Day 18: Ask Your Team What They Love Doing—Then Amplify It

Every team has hidden horsepower.

Ask each person:
"What do you love doing that we should use more?"

Listen.
Then act.
Restructure one task, one workflow, or one role to use that energy.

Passion is fuel. Use it.

Day 19: Some Processes Suck. Pick One. Add Pleasure. Build from There.

Pick one process your team repeats often—and everyone knows it sucks. Maybe it's flat, robotic, draining, or just unnecessary admin.

Shift it toward a pleasure focus.
Add a human touch.
Make the outcome matter. Celebrate progress.

Less miserable is not an outcome.
More alive is.

Rewiring processes—**from suckable to pleasurable**—creates energy that spreads.

Day 20: Reflect + Reset

What's shifted in the last four weeks?
List three things that feel clearer, faster, or stronger.

Then list one thing you'll keep cutting,
one thing you'll double down on,
and one new thing you'll test next cycle.

Momentum is easier to protect than rebuild—if you lead with intent.

Final Sequence: Lock + Launch

The sprint is done.
Now you lock what worked—
and build your rhythm for the next 30 days.
This is where short-term resets become long-term results.

Day 21: Lock the Ritual

Don't let the reset fade into another forgotten sprint.
Look back and identify the one ritual—daily, weekly, or strategic—that changed the game for you or your team.

Name it. Share it. Protect it.

Lock it in as non-negotiable.
Rituals beat reminders.
That's how real change sticks.

Day 22: Commit to the Next 30

Resets age like milk. Not like single cask, single pot still Irish whiskey.

What matters is the rhythm you build after.
Declare your next 30-day cycle.

What's the mission now?
What's the new 20% you're protecting?
Set your next sharp focus—then lead like a producer.

Every film wraps.
The next one rolls.
The team levels up.
The system resets.

That's how pros lead. Cycle by cycle.
Clarity first. Momentum always.

Leading Through the Reset

How to Run It, What to Avoid, and How to Lock It In

You've Got the Playbook. Now Lead It.

This Playbook is a leadership system for getting shit done. Cutting what's holding you back and fixing what's worth keeping but not working.

What this is not, is it is neither a strategy doc nor a set of suggestions. It's a playbook for how you lead execution—live, daily, in motion.

What you do with it now is what defines your team's trajectory.

Run It With the Team

Execution shifts when teams move together, under clear direction, led with intent.

Start simple:

- **Kick it off clearly.**
  Set the stage. One outcome per week. One move per day.
- **Use short pulses.**
  10-minute syncs beat 60-minute check-ins.
- **Model the move.**
  If you're not living the reset, they won't either.

You are the standard. If you break it, they will too.

Avoid the Classic Traps

This system works—if you don't sabotage it.
Here's what kills execution resets:

- **Overengineering:**
  It's one move per day, not a summit.
- **Skipping days:**
  Miss one, fine. Miss three, and the rhythm's broken.
- **Hiding the move:**
  If you believe in the reset, lead it out loud.
  Don't keep it quiet, test it in secret, or drip-feed it later.
  Bring your team in from the outset and move.

And the biggest one?

Waiting until things are bad to start.
Start now.
While you still have control.

The Serial Spark Sequence

Can't run a full reset right now?
No problem.

Start with five days. One bottleneck. Full focus.

The **Serial Spark Sequence** is an ignition system.
It fires fast, hits one friction point hard, and clears space fast.

Test traction, unlock early momentum, and fire up execution.

It's built for:

- ✓ Leaders who want to test traction fast—without overwhelming the team
- ✓ Teams already jammed who need a clean entry point
- ✓ Moments when execution is stuck and you need a breakthrough now

Run it with a pilot group.
Run it with your whole team.
What matters is that, big or small, you **spark the move.**

What It Looks Like

Here's the basic sequence:

- ▹ **Day 1: Identify the friction** – Pinpoint the single biggest bottleneck slowing execution for your team.
- ▹ **Day 2: Map the impact** – Get clear on what it's costing (lost time, energy, money, or momentum).
- ▹ **Day 3: Design the move** – Define the one shift that would create the biggest improvement, fast.
- ▹ **Day 4: Execute and embed** – Implement the fix and build a micro-ritual to lock it in.
- ▹ **Day 5: Debrief and decide what sticks** – Review what changed, what worked, and whether it's worth scaling up.

One team. One problem.
One week to shift momentum.

Use it as a tactical strike—or as the front door to the full 30-Day Reset.

Leading a team and want help running it?
Reach out.
No pitch. **No cost.**
Just precision.

> **Five days.**
> **Thirty minutes a day.**
> **One-on-one.**

You invested in *The 20% Leader*—we'll back your next move.

The Serial Spark Sequence is fully unlocked and fee waived for book buyers.

No pitch.
No pressure.
Just precision support to help you lead sharper.

> *(For full transparency, we normally charge a nominal fee for this—and although it's fully refundable, in your case, it's removed. Let's be honest: the refund exists purely to guarantee satisfaction. The focus isn't on fees. It's on traction. For us, Serial Spark Sequences are about value, not barriers.)*

Note: Serial Spark Sessions are designed for leaders with teams. Always fee free to reach out. If you're still in the process of building yours and ready to lead with intent, reach out and we'll explore if it's a fit.

Running The Execution Playbook

Once you've reset execution, you need to run it forward.

> **That's what Chapter 7 is about:**
> **Real-time execution rhythm.**
> **Live dashboards. One-screen focus.**
> A system that scales clarity and speed—without adding bulk.

Ready to make it permanent?
Let's build the system that makes it stick.

Chapter Seven

The Execution Playbook

Build a System That Drives Results—Without Driving You Crazy

The reset got you moving.
Now it's time to build the system that keeps you moving—without slowing you down.

This is where most leaders screw it up.
They overcomplicate. Add dashboards.
Layer in tech, and somehow end up slower than when they started.

Execution doesn't need more inputs.
It needs fewer *moving parts*—and more *moving outcomes.*

This chapter shows you how to build an execution rhythm your team can run in real time.

Fast. Visual. Frictionless.

No spreadsheets.
No micromanagement.
No bullshit.

One-Screen Execution

Cut the Clutter. Lead from a Single View.

You can't drive clarity when your team is scattered across 12 tabs and 7 tools. If your **focus** lives in one place, your **blockers** in another, and your **results** in a third—you've already lost.

You don't need more data. You need **one clean view:**

- What matters now
- Who's moving it forward
- What's in the way
- And how close you are to winning

That's the **one-screen rule:**

> **If it doesn't fit on one screen, it doesn't belong in your daily execution circuit.**

We're about to build the execution cockpit your team actually wants to use.

What Belongs on the Screen

The one-screen rule about **discipline**, not design.
It forces you to strip execution down to what *actually* moves the business forward.

Here's what belongs—and nothing else:

The Core Outcome

What are we building in this quarter?
What's the one thing we're driving toward—right now?
Stated clearly. Measurable. Unmissable.

From there, break it down into what matters *this month, this week,* and *today*. This screen should carry all four levels of focus:

90-Day Objective

One strategic goal.
What this quarter is for.

Monthly Focus

The current milestone.
What progress looks like right now.

Weekly Priority

The needle-mover for this week
Where the pressure is applied.

Today's Move

The next divisible action.
Not a plan. Not a status update. A move.
Something real. Something happening now.

Blockers in Play

What's slowing you down—right now?
Tech issues. People gaps. Decisions stuck in limbo.
If it's not visible, it won't get fixed.

Ownership

Who's got the ball?
If there's no name next to it, it's already dropped.

That's it.
If you've got more than that, you're not executing—you're reporting.

Signal Over Status

Most dashboards are graveyards for updates no one reads.
They show what happened, not what's moving.

Even when they are flooded with live data—
but real-time **status** isn't the same as real-time **signal**.

A real execution screen shows **signal, not status**.

It answers one question:
Are we moving—or are we stuck?

Signal tells you what needs to move now.
Status tells you what's there.

That's the difference.

- Seeing stock levels in real time? That's *status*.
- Being alerted that a store is low and a reorder needs triggering? That's ***signal***.
- Tracking hours worked? *Status*.
- Seeing which project is lagging and needs a reset? ***Signal***.

If your screen just shows numbers, updates, or red-yellow-green traffic lights—it might be *live*, but it's not a dashboard—it's a delay.
It's dead weight unless it prompts action.

Build for Momentum, Not Memory

Don't display what's been done.
Display what must happen next.

A screen should drive decisions, not just display data.
Ask this:

"If no one looked at this screen, what wouldn't get done?"

If nothing breaks—strip it out.

What you want:

- ✓ Triggers, not trackers.
- ✓ Moves, not metrics.
- ✓ Direction, not decoration.

Want to test your screen? Ask this:
Could a team member walk up to it and know what to move, now?

If the answer's no—it's *status*.
If the answer's yes—it's ***signal***.

Build a screen people *use*—not one they admire.

Keep the Cognitive Load Low

The best execution screens take **seconds** to read. If it takes a team more than a glance to understand what's happening, it's too heavy.

Clarity isn't just visual.
It's **mental**.

Your screen should feel like a cockpit:

Fast inputs. Clear decisions. Shared direction.

One Screen = One Truth

If your team is checking three places to figure out what matters, they're not executing—they're guessing.

That screen becomes your **shared source of truth.**

Not a system of record.
A system of *action*.

One view. One focus. One direction.

The Live Leadership Circuit

Lead in real time—not from reports

Execution is a Circuit

Execution doesn't run in straight lines. Signals shift.
Priorities flex. Teams hit friction.
Execution cycles through dynamic phases.

When leaders treat execution like a linear plan, things break.
Momentum fades. Issues compound. Silence grows.

A *set and forget* mindset breaks the circuit.
It interrupts flow, feedback, and clarity.

High-performance leaders stay synced with the current.
They align with execution's natural rhythm—treating it like an **engagement circuit:** continuous, responsive, always moving.

That's why great leaders don't guess. They tune in.

Every engagement circuit runs on three signals:

1. **Signal** – What's happening right now?
2. **Sense** – What's off, what's moving, what's slowing down?
3. **Shift** – Where do I intervene or recalibrate?

If that circuit breaks, leadership becomes lagging.
You find out *after* the drop—not before it.

Visibility Without Micromanagement

You don't need a hundred updates.
You need a single source of truth that shows where energy is—and isn't.

When teams can see their own progress, they move faster.
When leaders can track execution at a glance, they lead cleaner.

Set visibility rules that cut the noise:

- **Progress lives in one place.** No chasing updates.
- **Ownership is named.** No ghost tasks.
- **Everyone sees the same screen.** No silos, no surprises.

Visibility is about momentum.
Weak leaders make it about surveillance.

When it's about momentum, visibility becomes a performance trigger (one that self corrects) and accountability becomes automatic.

Intervene Without Oversteering

When the circuit signals something's off—act.
But don't jump in with both feet.

Smart leaders know when to trim the sail—not snatch the wheel.

Check for drift:
Has clarity faded?
Is ownership unclear?
Is pace dropping?

Then step in *surgically*.
Ask.
Clarify.
Reset the frame.

Real leadership protects flow.

Control is already part of the job—you don't need to clutch it.
Course corrections are cleaner when done early and light.

Rhythm Over Reactivity

Execution needs a beat. Not a schedule—*a pulse*.
Fast enough to stay fresh. Light enough to keep moving.

Run two simple cadences:

1. **Weekly strategy pulse:**
   Anchor the week with one focus.
   No fluff. No stretch goals.
   One pressure point. Clear push.
   Every team aligned.

2. **Daily micro-checks:**
   5 minutes.
   What's moving? What's stuck?
   Less talking. More signal.
   Done standing up—or in the chat.

These aren't meetings.
They're tempo control.
They keep teams alive, aware, and aligned—
without dragging down the work.

Lock It In

From Dashboard to Daily Behaviour

Make Execution Visible, Daily, and Personal

Like driving a car—
people drive the car, the dashboard **signals** what matters.

Execution works the same way.
A petrol gauge says half full ... Meh—*status*. So what?
A petrol light flashes red—**signal** ... Time to move.

People don't take action because they saw a pie chart. They act when ownership is clear, feedback is real-time, and the scoreboard hits home.

Here's how to make it daily:

- **One-screen clarity:**
  What are we building, and what's the move today?
- **Name on every outcome:**
  No passengers. No shadow owners.
- **Live tension:**
  Every metric should create movement. If it doesn't, kill it.

Managing performance is a liability.
It's a cost centre.

Engineering momentum moves financials—
so build it in and make it inescapable.

Install the Weekly Execution Circuit

Your team doesn't need more meetings.

They need a cadence that keeps focus sharp, movement clean, momentum increasing and results real.

Here's how to keep execution in a circuit that stays hot and focused:

1. **Monday Morning - Set the Strike Zone:**
   What's the single move that matters this week?
   Lock it in. Frame it hard.
   Make it visible.

2. **Tuesday Afternoon - Check the Pulse:**
   Fast friction scan.
   What's stuck, who needs backup, and where are we drifting?

3. **Friday Midday - Call the Impact:**
   What moved? What didn't?
   What carries forward?

No decks.
No show-and-tells.
Just **movement checks.**

If you're not seeing traction by Friday, Monday was soft and you didn't lead hard enough.

Fix the circuit—or stop pretending you're executing.

Execution Sprints: Strategy That Hits the Ground

Forget task management.
That's admin.

Execution is about pressure-tested strikes that move the business forward.

Turn strategy into short, sharp campaigns:

- **30-day sprint.**
- **One clear outcome.**
- **Daily traction checks.**
- **Weekly pulse reviews.**
- **Named owner—no passengers.**

This isn't a roadmap review.
It's the work—moving, live, visible.

Here's the simple truth, naked and unabashed.
No one cares about your roadmap if it's not moving.

Execution Sprints lead with conviction and executed decisively show the map in motion.

If your strategy isn't hitting the ground in real time, you don't have a strategy. You have a wishlist.

Clarity Cascades & Priority Sprints: Micro-Moves with Massive Impact

When teams stall, it's not because they're lazy.
It's because clarity didn't make it past the leadership layer.

Clarity Cascades fix that—fast.

A Clarity Cascade is a top-down clarity strike that turns leadership intent into real-time execution—across every layer.

Think:

CEO → Exec → Department → Team → Individual.
One priority. One message. Zero ambiguity.

What a Clarity Cascade Is (High-Level View)

Here's what a strong Clarity Cascade delivers:

- ✓ What matters *right now.*
- ✓ How each team moves the mission.
- ✓ What gets cut to make room for speed.

What It Looks Like in Practice (Granular Breakdown)

- ▹ **Start at the top:**
  What's the one outcome we're driving *this quarter/month?*
- ▹ **Break it down:**
  What does each team/function need to deliver to move that forward?

- **Cut the noise:**
  What can be paused, scrapped, or postponed to clear the way?

- **Lock it in:**
  Write it. Share it. Show it. One page. One message. Zero ambiguity.

Avoid thinking of this as a brainstorm.
It's a **clarity strike**—from the top, through the middle, to the edges.

How to Run a Clarity Cascade (Execution Steps)

Forget meetings. This is a *messaging sequence*—anchored in one sharp insight and pushed through the layers fast.

Think: signal, translate, transmit.

- **Step 1: Leader locks the priority.**
  One outcome, one timeline—usually monthly or quarterly.

- **Step 2: Translate for function.**
  What does *each team* do to move this? Sales, ops, product, etc.

- **Step 3: Push the message.**
  One-page clarity drop via email, Slack, Loom, or live 10-minute sync.

- **Step 4: Confirm sync.**
  Team leads reflect it back. Not "got it"—but "here's what we're doing."

Timeframe: Can be executed in under 24 hours.
Rhythm: Best run monthly, or when shifting focus.

This is about **unified signal clarity.**
Alignment at speed.

What a Priority Sprint Is (High-Level View)

When one area is stuck or dragging—run a Priority Sprint:

- Target one stuck zone.
- Kill the competing noise.
- Rebuild momentum in real time.

Think of it like **triage for slow or slowing momentum.**

One function. One reset. One fast win.

What It Looks Like in Practice (Granular Breakdown)

- **Spot the drag:**
  What area's slowing momentum right now?
  Name the stuck zone.
- **Cut to the signal:**
  Ditch side quests.
  Focus on the one friction point that actually matters.
- **Define the shift:**
  What's the win you want in the next 7–10 days?
  Make it specific.
- **Tighten the circuit:**
  Run fast pulses—daily stand-ups, micro-checks, live fixes.
- **Lock the learnings:**
  Debrief hard.
  What moved? What worked? What gets scaled next?

How to Run a Priority Sprint (Execution Steps)

A **Priority Sprint** is a **focused strike** to reboot progress in a stuck area. Think of it as a fast intervention that restores flow where things are bogging down.

- **Step 1: Identify the stuck zone.**
  Could be a team, process, product line, or function.
- **Step 2: Strip it down.**
  What's dragging? Tools? Decisions? Comms? Clarity?
- **Step 3: Set one outcome.**
  One needle-mover for the next 7–10 days.
  No passengers.
- **Step 4: Run it live.**
  Daily 10-minute pulse
  (Slack, huddle, check-in).
- **Step 5: Debrief and lock in.**
  What moved? What sticks? What scales?

Timeframe: 7–10 days
Team: Cross-functional or within one unit
Context: When momentum stalls and you can't wait for the next big planning cycle

This is **leadership at tactical depth.**
No bloat. Just decisive, targeted reset.

Pin the Playbook

Don't shelf this.

Lock it in.
'Nail it to the wall.'
Make it visible.

Most leadership playbooks are conceptual. This isn't.
It's your new operating rhythm—*if you'll run it.*
Make it a ritual. Build the habit.

Post it. Walk it. Run it. *Daily.*
Make execution visible—so it becomes inescapable.

Here's how to make it real:

- ✓ **Print your one-screen execution view**—digital or physical.
  Put it where your team looks *every day.*
- ✓ **Map your weekly rhythm together.**
  10-minute kickoff Monday.
  Midweek signal check.
  Friday impact wrap. *Stick to it.*
- ✓ **Run a live Priority Sprint.**
  Rally the team.
  Name one friction point.
  Sketch the reset. *Then move.*

Execution gets real through rhythm and repetition—not ideas.
If it's not **seen**, it's not **run**.
If it's not **felt**, it won't **stick**.

Tactical Moves in Action

Mini-examples of the tools that make execution real

Following are some examples from the field and work I've done with clients.

Clarity Cascade

The CEO of a 40-person SaaS company locked the monthly priority:

"Increase trial-to-paid conversions by 20%."

She dropped a one-pager:

Sales focuses on tighter follow-ups.
Product optimises onboarding.
Marketing runs retargeting.

Each team lead reflected back their plan in Slack within 24 hours. Alignment done—no meetings required.

Result: 23% uplift in conversions by month-end.

Execution Sprint

A consulting firm's pipeline had stalled.

They launched a 30-day sprint:

> **One goal—book 20 high-leverage sales calls.**
> **Daily Slack updates tracked progress.**
> **Marketing supported with fresh outbound copy.**

Friday wrap: 17 booked. Lessons documented. One process changed permanently.

Priority Sprint

Customer support backlog doubled in 2 weeks.

COO kicked in a 10-day Priority Sprint with the support lead:

Outcome = Reduce backlog by 50%.

They paused lower-urgency requests, simplified ticket routing, and ran daily syncs. By Day 9, backlog was cleared and a new auto-triage rule is in place.

Result: Customer satisfaction scores jump by 18%. Response time halved.

Making It Stick

Sustainability, Reinforcement, and Real-World Rhythm

Keep Evolving or Start Dying

Execution isn't a sprint. It's not a campaign.
It's not a single initiative with a neat finish line.

Execution is a *system* ...
and systems either evolve—or degrade.

If you treated the 30-Day Reset like a burst of effort just to prove what's possible—think again.

It was your ignition point.
The moment you took back the wheel and reinstalled a new operating rhythm.

Now the real work begins.

Because clarity fades.
Momentum leaks.
And left alone, even the sharpest execution circuits start to wobble.

High-performance execution is **leadership in motion**—ongoing, adaptive, precise. It's not about going hard and hoping it sticks.

You don't lead execution once. You lead it again and again.
Reset the signal. Reinforce the rhythm. Rebuild the intensity.

Just like elite athletes revisit form, routine, and rhythm ...
Elite leaders revisit execution *daily*.

This is your new practice.
No end state. No autopilot. No arrival.
Execution lives or dies by the focus you give it.

See the Stall. Kill It Early

Stall-outs creep in unannounced.

Teams start drifting. Wheels spin.
Execution stalls. Momentum evaporates.
The pace dulls. Energy fades. Edges blur.

Sharp execution runs on rhythm.
If the rhythm weakens, momentum dies quietly.

Here's what to watch:

- **Circuits get looser.**
  Weekly pulses go soft. Check-ins stretch or vanish.
- **Language gets vague.**
  "We're still looking at..." replaces clear next moves.
- **Ownership gets muddy.**
  Actions float—no name, no drive.
- **Focus splinters.**
  One priority becomes three. Then five. Then confusion.

Want to know if your team's slipping?

Ask these four on Friday—every Friday:

- What actually moved this week?
- Where did energy slow or stall?
- What got talked about—but not touched?
- What did we do that should've been deleted?

Keep your radar tuned.
Don't wait for the break.
Intervene before inertia hardens.

If you don't measure momentum, you'll only notice it when it's gone
Ignore the stall and you're signing up for a rebuild.

Kill the Comeback of Chaos

Stop the slide before momentum disappears

Snapback creeps in like comfort—but feels like a sledgehammer.
That's life. Incremental losses hit hard when you finally notice them.

Old habits don't just reappear.
They drift in when you stop paying attention.

It's the little things:
The meeting gets skipped.
The check-in goes soft.
The focus blurs.

And suddenly, you're back where you started.

Think of it like weight loss:

You drop 10kg, but your body remembers being 20kg heavier. You haven't built the synaptic bridges that see you as fit and healthy—at least not stronger than the old ones that see you as overweight.

> If those new neural paths don't take over,
> the old ones become the default.
> It's not about willpower.
> It's about memory—neural, behavioural, operational.

Execution works the same way.
You built the new system.
Now you have to **defend it. Embed it.**
Make it the only choice—not just the primary one.

Here's what triggers the slide:

- **New projects pile on:**
  Everything's working—so you say yes to more.
  The calendar bloats. Pressure rises. Systems strain.

- **Team changes:**
  A new hire. A key exit. A shift in leadership.
  Momentum wobbles before anyone notices.

- **Leader fatigue:**
  You lead a high-performance team—but neglect your own baseline. Without practices that reset you on the fly (Transcendental Meditation, breathwork, micro-journaling, movement), you ease up "just for a week." Then clarity fades. Ownership slips. The circuit stalls.

How to hold the line:

- **Lock your pulses:**
  Monday's 10-minute kickoff?
  Guard it. Don't let it bloat into a deck-driven time suck.

- **Walk the wall:**
  The execution playbook should live where the team works.

  Seen = repeated. Repeated = sustained.

- **Audit monthly**
  Ask: What crept back in? What got soft?
  What needs to be cut—again?

Snapback is natural.
It's what happens when nothing holds the new standard in place.

So build the friction. Install the anchors. Defend the reset.
Because once it starts slipping—it doesn't stop.
Unless you stop it.

Ritualise the Rhythm. Codify the Momentum.

Clarity fades. Momentum leaks.
Rituals are how you hold the line.

Rituals don't just anchor rhythm.
They **build culture through repetition.**

But only if they're protected—and enforced.

You've already built the circuit.
Now you make it unbreakable.

This isn't about adding more check-ins.
It's about protecting the few you already run—
and making them *untouchable*.

Ask yourself:

- Is the Monday Kickoff locked in *everyone's* calendar?
- Is the Signal Check being skipped—or sharpened?
- Is the Friday Wrap surfacing impact—or hiding it?

Here's how to know they're working:

- **Monday Kickoff:**
  Is it just on the calendar,
  or are people showing up sharp and aligned?
  Are blockers being cleared fast—or rehashed week after week?
- **Midweek Signal Check:**
  Has the strike zone gone dark—
  or are we still locked and loaded?

  When the midweek signal is softer than erectile dysfunction and the energy's missing, momentum's already leaking—and you're no longer in the game, you're just playing dress-up.
- **Friday Impact Wrap:**
  Is it surfacing real movement—or just a status parade?
  Can your team articulate what actually improved?

These are your execution pulses.
Lose one, and the rhythm weakens.
Let two slip, and momentum snaps.

Rituals fail the moment they're no longer enforced.

It's like rust on a car. Ignore it once, and it spreads.
By the time you notice the bubble, it's already eaten through the frame.

Or like scuffed shoes you don't polish.
The wear compounds—until "shabby" becomes your new standard.

Don't let that happen here.
Catch the drift fast. Reinforce the standard.
Make the ritual sacred. *Or expect it to die quietly.*

Bottomline:
Rituals only work when they're **protected, respected, and enforced.**
If it slips once, it'll slip again.

Don't overthink it. **Just codify the circuit.**
Run it. Defend it. Let it build the culture.

Keep It Moving: Your 90-Day Continuity Plan

You've reset execution. You've locked the circuit.
Now it's time to **build the flywheel** that keeps momentum alive—without another breakdown and rebuild.

This is where 30 days turns into 90.
Where reset becomes rhythm.
And where execution shifts from "project" to operating system.

Run It Again, Smarter

The 30-Day Reset isn't a box you tick—
it's a leadership tool you **pull deliberately** to stay sharp and keep movement clean.

It's not a one-off.
It's a repeatable strike.

Depending on the scope of your team and your span of control, you may:

- Run it **across one team per quarter.**
- Target **one execution pillar** (clarity, speed, ownership).
- Lead **multiple parallel resets** if the organisation can absorb it.

Scale the reset to match the reality.
Whether it's one team or five—**you lead the rhythm.**

Codify Your Execution Operating System

You've codified your project-level circuit.
Now codify your **operating system.**

Your Execution Operating System isn't software—
it's how your team moves.

It's rhythm, clarity, ownership, and signal—codified and repeatable.

Capture it so execution doesn't live in memory—it lives in motion.

Write down and share:

- ▹ **Your one-screen execution view.**
- ▹ **The weekly circuit**
  (Monday kick-off, midweek signal, Friday wrap).
- ▹ **Clarity cascades and priority sprint.s**
- ▹ **Live momentum metrics** that show movement in real time.

What was a playbook becomes the **operating standard.**
This is about reinforcement because you're codifying a mechanism, instead of a moment.

Put it in writing. Make it visible. Own it across layers.

Schedule a Strategic Look-Back

Every 90 days, pause with purpose.
This isn't just about results. It's about execution **quality**.

Ask:

- ▹ What moved faster?
- ▹ What dragged or got messy?
- ▹ What crept back in?
- ▹ What sharpened results?

Get feedback. Capture signal. Then recalibrate.

This is a systems-level look at how well your execution engine is performing—and what needs tuning next.

Momentum Requires Intentional Force

Whether you are growing, scaling or locking in sustainable profits, execution is a flywheel.

To keep it spinning, you need to maintain momentum, and that means to **increase the mass** (**what moves**) and/or **tighten the velocity** (**how fast it moves**).

Mass might mean:

- More customers.
- More impact.
- Bigger plays.
- Sharper projects.

Velocity might mean:

- Faster cycles.
- Tighter feedback.
- Cleaner ownership.
- Better signal flow.

No business achieves operational inertia.

There is always a frequency, a cycle, a rhythm—and it's momentum that rides the rhythm through the cycles on the peaks and troughs of the frequency.

Momentum doesn't sustain itself.
It grows through strategic **velocity and mass**—not pressure.

More aligned action.
More clarity.
More clean motion.

If you want execution to stay sharp:

- Keep the circuits tight.
- Keep the system visible.
- Keep your leadership active.

Momentum degrades quietly.
Your job is to see it early—and respond decisively.

You don't keep momentum by pushing harder.
You keep it by building smarter.

> Reset before it stalls.
> Refine before it slips.
> Reinforce before it fades.
> **Reset before it's needed.**

That's how execution becomes scalable.
That's how momentum compounds.
That's how it becomes your new normal.
That's how leaders drive impact at the level that actually matters.

Chapter Eight

Finish Sharp. Move Forward.

Execution compounds.
Leadership never clocks out.

Execution Is an Infinite Circuit of Evolution

Just like life is about the journey, the reset was always meant to be ignition.

This was never about a fixed destination.
It was a milestone on a longer path.

The good news is that the heavy lifting is done.
Now you get to have the real fun with it as you elevate it and the business and lead from a higher plane.

You've built the rhythm, installed the circuit, and clarified the moves.

Now you lead through momentum.
You keep it alive, visible, and real—through how your team moves each day, with clarity, ownership, and velocity.
Not in planning rooms.
Not in spreadsheets.

The strongest leaders stay close to the signal.
When they pause, it's strategic—fuel for the next move.

They keep execution hot.
Their presence reinforces authority.
It reminds the team:
You're in the right seat—and so are they.

Leadership Is a Choice You Keep Making

Leadership doesn't begin when you get promoted.
It begins the moment you choose to take ownership—then keep choosing.

Because leadership isn't a title. It's a choice you make every day, under pressure, in motion, when no one's watching.

Your team doesn't follow your job description.
They follow your energy. Your clarity. Your follow-through.

They watch what you tolerate.
They mirror what you prioritise.
They respond to what you signal—consistently.

Leadership isn't about charm.
It's not about presence.

It's about *follow-through under fire.*
The choice to drive clarity instead of blame.
To set the tempo instead of waiting for consensus.
To keep the pressure clean—even when it's inconvenient.

If you want a stronger team, make stronger leadership choices.
And keep making them. Every day.

What Got You Here Isn't What Gets You Next

Resetting execution was the shift.
Sustaining it—**while growing it**—is the next level.

You're no longer just making moves.
You're shaping a team that moves on its own.
You're building leaders who operate at speed.
You're installing execution as culture.

This next phase is about:

- **Raising the floor**
  Making high-performance the new baseline.
- **Expanding the edge**
  Taking bigger swings with cleaner execution.
- **Scaling the signal**
  Helping your leaders lead the same way.

Leadership at this level is about doing less—with more precision, clarity, and conviction.

Avoid the temptation to just take on more because you think you can, when you increase mass do it strategically or momentum will slow.

You now have a system. Protect it. Elevate it.
And empower your people to run with it.
Because the business doesn't need a new plan.
It needs stronger execution energy flowing through every layer.

Execution Is Also the Mirror of Leadership

You want to know who the real leader is?
Don't look at the org chart.
Look at the execution.

Because execution is:
Where strategy, culture, and credibility collide.
Where clarity either translates—or dies.
Where influence either sticks—or fades.
Where values either show up—or fall flat.

Every missed deliverable, every vague update, every piece of stalled momentum?

It's not just a systems issue.
It's a *signal issue.*

Your leadership shows up in the pace, sharpness, and ownership of the team because you shape the how of the work that is done.

Like numbers on the company financials, execution doesn't lie.
It tells you what's real, and if you're willing to look at it—it will tell you what to fix.

Because at the end of the day, **execution is the scoreboard of leadership.**

It either ships clean—or it doesn't.
Leadership owns that.

The Team Always Moves at the Speed of the Leader

For decades, leadership training taught managers to become glorified cheerleaders. It worked—to a point.

Morale lifted.
Collaboration improved.
But something else crept in.

Entitlement.
Inflated self-importance.
A creeping fear of saying the wrong thing.

Leadership became cautious.
Over-accommodating.
Dull when it needed to cut clean.

It wasn't all bad—contrast fuels evolution and now, it's time to course-correct.

Teams need signal clarity. Strategic challenges coupled with just enough resistance so that they push and grow.

They need real energy.
And that starts with you.

Your pace is their pace.
Your focus becomes their focus.
If you drift—they drift.
If you dull the edge—they'll blunt the blade.
If you move sharp, clean, and clear—they'll match you.

This doesn't mean doing the work for them.
It means leading in a way that leaves no confusion:

- What matters now.
- Where we're going.
- What we're cutting.
- How we move.

This is leadership:
Tempo. Tone. Terrain.

No one rises higher than the signal you send.
So send a clean one.
And keep sending it.

Spot Drift. Cut Fast.

Execution failure is easy to spot—**if you're looking.**

Picture a drunk in a bright Hawaiian shirt who's just lost everything but the shirt, stumbling out of a casino at 5am and face-planting into the pavement.

You can't miss it—unless you're looking the other way.

Execution is like that.
It slips. Quietly. Then repeatedly.
Eventually, the new standard becomes
"just get it done" instead of *"get it done right."*

The shift is subtle:

- Sharp check-ins get padded with noise
- Faux priorities multiply, real urgencies get ignored—but no one notices
- Everyone's busy, but progress feels slow
- Ownership gets implied instead of named

That's not chaos.
That's **drift**—and drift compounds fast.

High-performance execution demands high-frequency awareness.
When you feel the rhythm loosening, act immediately and decisively.
When sharp edges go dull, no matter what the reason, don't excuse it.

If you lead with accountability and your team chooses to follow then they can be held accountable. This is where the distinction between accountability and the lesser responsibility becomes acute.

Intervene early. Cut clean. Reset fast.

Don't wait until momentum collapses.
Catch the shift before the stall.
In execution, drift doesn't ask permission.

Speed saves. Clarity recovers. Precision prevents.

Set the Energy Standard

Leadership is many things.
Strategy sets direction. Culture sets tone.
But operationally?
It's signal, and **your energy is the first transmission.**

People don't just listen to what you say.
They tune into how you show up.

Are you sharp—or scattered?
Present—or distracted?
Focused—or floating?

The team calibrates off you.

You don't have to be loud.
You don't have to be extroverted.
But you do have to bring signal strength—consistently.

Because when leadership energy fades, the team slows down and, often worse, they start guessing; and when they start guessing, **clarity dies** and **execution leaks.**

Your Energy Speaks First:

- ▹ You don't need hype—you need presence.
- ▹ You don't need charisma—you need conviction.
- ▹ You don't need to have the answers—you need to move with intent.

When you show up clean and clear, the signal stabilises.
When you drift or dilute, the system wobbles.

Set the tone.
Set the tempo.
Set the energy standard.

Because if you don't, something—or someone—else will.

Precision Trumps Time Every Time

Leaders who use the excuse that they failed because they ran out of time are simply sloppy.

They failed because they wasted time on the wrong things.
Time gets blamed. Precision is what's missing.

Every hour spent in rework is a symptom of fuzzy direction.
Every dropped task is a symptom of invisible ownership.
Every sprint that ends in "almost done"
is a sign that no one set the strike zone.

This has zero to do with hustle and everything to do with *cutting clean*—and aiming sharp.

If your team is always flat out but nothing's moving, zoom out:

- What are we chasing that no longer matters?
- What's on the calendar that adds zero velocity?
- Who's running in circles because no one clarified the next move?

Precision cuts fast.
Precision creates leverage.
Precision tells your team: *"We move this, now."*

The most dangerous lie in leadership is: *"We just need more time."*

No. You need to lead with sharper signal.
Tighter circuits. Cleaner execution.

Speed isn't the issue. Direction is.

So don't push harder.
Lead sharper.

This Book Was Never About Process. It's About Presence.

Looking for something to add to your bookshelf for 'another time'?

This ain't it!

With this you now have a system that cuts through the noise.
Not something to study—something to use.
It's a leadership mechanism to run, daily.
Now you need to lead like you mean it.

The 20% Leader isn't a role or a title.
It's how you lead when you bring clarity, move outcomes, and sharpen the team through action.

If you've got all the answers, you're not leading—
you're the subject matter expert.
That's a different job.

As a leader, your job isn't to know everything.
It's to **spot bullshit fast, hold the line, and keep things moving.**

You don't need to be the smartest person in the room.
You just need to lead like you belong at the front of the room.

Stand in the pocket.
Lead with conviction.
Hold the standard.

Execution lives or dies by presence.
Not posture. Not platitudes.
Presence.

- Are you visible where it counts?
- Are you showing up with real energy?
- Are you reinforcing the rhythm you helped install?

The team doesn't need perfection.
They need a leader who's locked in and *moves with purpose.*

This book was built to deliver that.
Not fluff. Not theory.

A system of clarity, leverage, and live leadership.

You've got the moves now.
Make them yours.
And keep them moving.

Final Note: Don't Lead Alone

Even the sharpest leaders use outside clarity to stay on edge.

They spot drift faster. Tighten signal earlier. Protect momentum when it matters most.

But not all support is equal.

There are **networking groups**—
and then there are *rooms worth being in.*
The right ones challenge your thinking, not just your schedule.

For emerging leaders, broad access matters.
General leadership networks can provide exposure, insight, and inspiration. But choose them wisely—where you stand now isn't where you plan to stay.

For advancing leaders, the bar is higher.
You need **peer-based masterminds** with real accountability and strategic stretch. A room full of yes-men won't sharpen your edge.

For senior and enterprise-level leaders, exclusivity is the filter.
You need environments where context is already understood—and every minute counts. business clubs, high-stakes masterminds, and precision interactive engagement circuits become non-negotiable.

Wherever you sit—**surround yourself with sharp minds and shared standards**. Because leadership can get lonely fast. And drift doesn't wait for permission.

So what's next?

That depends on where you are, and where you lead from.

Whether you're leading 5 or 500, what matters most is that you have:

- A way to challenge your perspective
- An engagement circuit that keeps you sharp
- A trusted sounding board to call signal from noise

Find your room.
Find your rhythm.
Then move like it matters.

If you've been running this reset—or plan to—and want precision support as you lead through the next phase, you're welcome to reach out.

No pitch. No pressure.

Just high-trust, one-to-one conversations with leaders who play the long game.

www.manolutions.com
(For clarity. For execution. For scale.)

Hope is a poor man's gambling addiction
The 20% Leader doesn't hope for results. He creates them.
Then he does it again tomorrow.

Chapter Nine

The 20% Leader's Tactical Mirror

**Don't pick. Don't dabble.
Run the whole system.**

These tools aren't tips.
They're how high-performance leaders build real momentum—day in, day out. They're the rhythm, signal, and structure that drive real execution.

If you've made it this far, you've already done more than most.

Now you have a choice.
Use what's here—and turn it into traction.
Or flick to the next idea, the next book,
the next "one day I'll use this" download.

Either way, choose.
Because leaders who drift are leaders who stall.
Momentum doesn't come from thinking. It comes from moving.

This book won't care if you use it.
But your business will. Your team will.
You will.

So don't dip your toe like a nervous tourist at the edge of the surf for the first time.

Dive in. Get wet.
Run the system.

Move like a leader—or don't bother calling yourself one.

And if that offends you, pause.
Because the words aren't the problem—your identity is.

A real leader reads that and nods.
An aspiring one feels the heat. That's the point.

This is the moment. You either shift—or you stall.

So make the call.
Step in. Or walk away.
Just don't pretend you didn't see the mirror.

Chapter Ten

Want Help Applying This?

If you've read this book and you're ready to run your own **Serial Spark Sequence**—the fast, focused version of the reset—we've got something for you.

Normally the Serial Spark Sequence is $100 (refundable or credited toward coaching if you choose to continue). But since you've already purchased *The 20% Leader*, we're waiving that fee—no strings attached.

> Just email your purchase receipt to support@manolutions.com and we'll book you straight in.

No funnel. No pitch. Just help.

> ***Heads-up:*** *These sessions are for leaders with teams, targets, and traction. If you're still getting those in place, no problem reaching out—if we think it's the right move, we'll lock in the sessions. If it's too early, we'll help point you in the right direction.*

Chapter Eleven

The 20% Leader's Tactical Toolkit

This is your tactical toolkit. The execution system broken into parts. Use all of it—no skipping, no cherry-picking.

Leaders don't guess.
They install rhythm, pressure, and clarity.
This is how.

JFK's Clarity Model

Why it matters: Sharpens vision, simplifies direction.

Use it when: Your team's unclear on what matters most.

Structure:

- What do I really want?
- Why does it matter?
- What does done look like?

Commander's Intent

Why it matters: Removes decision bottlenecks, builds autonomy.

Use it when: You want speed without chaos.

Structure:

- Outcome: What are we trying to achieve?
- Context: Why does it matter?
- Boundaries: What's non-negotiable?

Execution Sprint

Why it matters: Converts strategy into momentum fast.

Use it when: You want sharp, time-bound traction.

Structure:

- 30 days
- One outcome
- Daily checks
- Weekly pulse
- Named owner

Clarity Cascade

Why it matters: Drives top-down alignment without meetings.

Use it when: You're shifting focus or rolling out strategy.

Steps:

- Lock the priority
- Translate by function
- Push message
- Confirm sync

Priority Sprint

Why it matters: Kills drag and restarts stuck areas.

Use it when: A team or project loses momentum.

Structure:

- Identify stuck zone
- Cut noise
- Set 7–10 day goal
- Run live
- Lock the learning

One-Screen Execution View

Why it matters: Gives instant clarity and ownership.

Use it when: Teams are scattered or chasing ghosts.

Must include:

- 90-day goal
- Weekly focus
- Today's move
- Blockers + ownership

Weekly Execution Circuit

Why it matters: Locks momentum into rhythm.

Use it when: Teams drift or execution loses edge.

Flow:

- Monday: Set the strike zone
- Tuesday: Check the pulse
- Friday: Call the impact

Chapter Twelve

The 20% Leader's Energy Toolkit

The Frequency Ladder for Leaders

What you feel is how you lead.

Emotional state sets the tone for the entire room.
Like it? Hate it?
Doesn't matter.
You won't escape it.

This isn't abstract woo-woo theory—
it's observable reality.

When you lead from fear, anger, or scarcity, you get tension, withdrawal, short-term panic, and other negative reactions.

When you lead from clarity, courage, or purpose—
you get execution and you create movement.

Using the lens of the ***20% Leader***, this ladder adapts the *Map of Consciousness* developed by **Dr. David R. Hawkins**, author of *Power vs. Force*. Hawkins proposed that every emotional state carries a measurable frequency.

The numbers are up for debate.
The patterns aren't.

In practice, I've found this to be 100% accurate in every underperforming leadership team I've worked with since first reading *'Power vs. Force'* in 1995.

Use this ladder as a diagnostic and directional guide.

Where are you operating from right now?
What is that frequency creating in your culture?
What is it costing—or compounding?

Low States: Friction, Force, and Fallout

Level 20: Shame

Avoids visibility. Deflects decisions.

Crystallises into self-erasure and inner retreat.

Solidifies into a culture of silence.

What follows: No one speaks up. Nothing moves.

Level 30: Guilt

Over-apologises. Second-guesses everything.

Crystallises into hesitation and emotional leakage.

Solidifies into lost opportunities.

What follows: Eroded confidence and indecision at every level.

Level 50: Apathy

Checked out. Doesn't care.

Crystallises into disengagement and quiet quitting.

Solidifies into stagnation.

What follows: Performance dies. Dead weight builds up.

Level 75: Grief

Stuck in what's broken. Can't move forward.

Crystallises into emotional residue and backward focus.

Solidifies into paralysis.

What follows: Past pain becomes present culture.

Level 100: Fear

Controls everything. Won't delegate.

Crystallises into obsessive overreach and caution loops.

Solidifies into micromanagement.

What follows: Team suffocates. Burnout spreads.

Level 125: Desire

Grasps at results. Chases every shiny thing.

Crystallises into attachment to outcomes.

Solidifies into disconnection.

What follows: Fatigue sets in. Trust breaks down.

Level 150: Anger

Reacts fast. Listens slow.

Crystallises into control struggles and emotional volatility.

Solidifies into intimidation.

What follows: Creativity collapses. Morale tanks.

Level 175: Pride

Needs to be right. Rejects feedback.

Crystallises into identity attachment and brittle confidence.

Solidifies into ego-driven leadership.

What follows: Learning stops. Culture freezes.

Mid States: Functioning but Flat

Level 200: Courage

Steps up. Owns the hard calls.

Crystallises into activated potential and real accountability.

Solidifies into action bias.

What follows: Progress starts. Energy builds.

Level 250: Neutrality

Stays calm. Avoids drama.

Crystallises into emotional detachment and situational steadiness.

Solidifies into stability.

What follows: Safe space, steady outcomes.

Level 310: Willingness

Leans in. Asks, not resists.

Crystallises into openness and growth orientation.

Solidifies into coachability.

What follows: Growth mindset becomes team DNA.

Level 350: Acceptance

Works with what is. Adapts fast.

Crystallises into flow readiness and response flexibility.

Solidifies into resilience.

What follows: Change becomes movement—not chaos.

Level 400: Reason

Thinks clearly. Cuts through noise.

Crystallises into sharp analysis and grounded strategy.

Solidifies into sound judgment.

What follows: Better decisions, faster progress.

> ***Consistent operators begin to evolve into strategic thinkers.***

High States: Multipliers, Not Managers

Level 500: Purpose-Driven

Leads with meaning. Aligns others to mission.

Crystallises into shared mission and intrinsic motivation.

Solidifies into teams that care deeply about the outcome.

What follows: People care more—and act faster.

> ***Belief scales. New leaders start to rise. Movements begin.***

Level 540: Energising

Lifts rooms. Transmits belief.

Crystallises into contagious energy and cultural lift.

Solidifies into cultural momentum.

What follows: Teams move without needing to be pushed.

> ***Energy compounds.***
> ***Emerging leaders start pulling others forward.***

Level 600: Strategic Calm

Sees the system. Moves without noise.

Crystallises into calm clarity and pattern recognition.

Solidifies into clarity under pressure.

What follows: Complexity simplifies. Teams execute cleanly.

> ***Decentralised leadership thrives.***
> ***Clarity spreads without chaos.***

Level 700+: Visionary

Thinks beyond today. Inspires without effort.

Crystallises into long-horizon clarity and decisive insight.

Solidifies into magnetic leadership.

What follows: People follow—not because they have to, but because they want to.

> ***Legacy-level leadership takes root.***

A print-friendly version of this can be downloaded at https://20percentleader.com/resources

Use It Like This

This isn't a personality quiz or some external badge to collect.

It's an *inner calibration tool*—an intrinsic check on how you're actually showing up. Misunderstand this as an extrinsic challenge, and you miss the point.

It's not a war on the outside. It's a quiet, daily war within—one that decides how far you'll go. Check yourself daily.

> *"Victorious warriors win first and then go to war, while defeated warriors go to war first and then seek to win."*
>
> *—Sun Tzu, The Art of War*

Ask yourself:

- Where am I actually leading from right now?
- What would shift if I climbed one level higher—just one?

Then act:

- Climb one level higher today.
- Catch yourself when you drop.
- Build frequency awareness like a skill, not a sermon.

You don't need to reach the top to lead better.
You just need to move up from where you are.

Crystallise better thoughts.
Solidify stronger habits—in yourself, and across your team.
That's how you shift your state—and shape your team.

You can't fake high-frequency leadership.
But you can train it.

Build the awareness.
Then build the muscle.

Organisational Setpoints

Your team has a baseline energy.

It's not what you write on the wall—
it's what shows up under pressure.

This is your organisational setpoint.

Not the best day.
Not the worst day.
The default state your team drops into when no one's looking.

Use It Like This:

1. **Name the Setpoint.**
   - Ask: *What do we default to under stress or silence?*
   - Is it calm? Chaos? Cynicism? Drive?
2. **Spot the Signal.**
   Look for these quick tells:
   - How fast do people bounce back after friction?
   - Are updates energy-giving or energy-draining?
   - Is there tension in the room—or traction?
3. **Reset the Tone.**
   Forget workshops. Just shift the rhythm:
   - Open weekly planning with:
     "What are we proud of?".
     It's an example. There are many more options.

- Run fast engagement circuits—
  celebrate progress in motion.
- Kill the zombie projects.
  Dead energy drags everyone down.

4. **Keep It Visible.**
   - Write your observed setpoint on the board.
   - Revisit monthly.
   - Raise the question:
     Is this who we are—or just what we've settled for?

Reality Check:
If your team moves like a daily slog, don't blame the workload.

That's the setpoint talking.
Reset the energy, and you reset the output.

Tools for Emotional Elevation

You can't lead from a state you haven't stepped into.

Your emotional state isn't fixed.
It's adjustable—*if you've got the tools to shift it fast.*

These aren't wellness routines.
They're tactical resets for leaders under pressure.
Micro-tools to help you climb the ladder, lead stronger, and stay sharp when things get messy.

You don't need an offsite.
You need tools that *work under pressure.*

Use It Like This:

When your energy drops, don't wait.
Use one of these to shift state—fast.

The 17-Second Reset

Hold a clear, elevated thought for 17 seconds.
Hold it for 68 seconds (4x17) and your focus compounds.
Thoughts click. Tone changes. Presence shifts.

Use this before a tough call, meeting, or pitch—
or anytime your energy is off.

It's simple. It works.

Clarity Anchors

Use a physical cue to snap back into clarity:

- Straighten posture.
- Breathe in calm.
- Touch a grounding object (ring, pen, notebook).
- Link it to a thought: *I move with clarity. I own the tone.*

Leader Signal Check

Ask in real time: *"What am I broadcasting right now?"*
If it's fear, stress, or control—pause.
Reset. Re-engage.

You set the tone.
If your signal's off, the room follows.

Momentum Cues: Empower Your Leaders to Drive the Shift

Once you've tested these tools—pass them on.
Your job isn't to carry the energy.
It's to **ignite it across the system.**

Equip your team leads and managers to drive energy in their own spaces:

- **Open meetings with motion.**
  Ask: *"What's already working?"*
- **Close on progress.**
  One clear momentum marker—always.
- **Kill the drag.**
  Name and shut down zombie projects early.
  Dead weight kills execution.

Your habits shape their horizon.
That's the silent message:
This is how we show up here.
Start by leading it.
Then hand it off—on purpose.

Elevation doesn't scale through inspiration.
It scales through ownership.

You can't lead from clarity if you're radiating chaos.

Train elevation like a skill. Use it on command. Then spread it.
Lead elevated.
Watch your team rise.

About the Author

Paul Lange is a high-performance strategist, leadership coach, and founder of **Manolutions**—a business optimisation firm built for leaders who want to scale with precision, clarity, and impact.

With more than 35 years across private equity, venture capital, and startup advisory, Paul has worked with hundreds of founders, executives, and operational leaders. He's helped sharpen strategy, scale systems, and build execution cultures that deliver serious bottom-line results.

He's the architect of **Total QX** (Total Quality Experience)—a proprietary performance framework that fuses leadership alignment, execution rhythm, and clarity-led transformation.

It's the engine behind his coaching programs and accredited leadership and management training pathways offered through his company Manolutions.

Paul doesn't theorise execution—he engineers it.

His work merges strategy, psychology, and signal clarity into a leadership model that moves fast, cuts clean, and scales sharp.

From emerging leaders to executive mastery, his programs are built for those who want to lead like it matters and execute like there's no Plan B.

When he's not advising boards or running intensives, Paul can be found on a bike, in the kitchen, or deep in Transcendental Meditation.

His Hedonist Entrepreneur philosophy blends pleasure, passion, purpose, and performance—because success should be both wildly profitable and deeply satisfying.

To learn more or explore working together, visit **manolutions.com**.

Also by Paul Lange

More Manolutions Publishing Titles

MIS(TRÈS)S ENTREPRENEUR MANIFESTO

Edge. Torque. Integrity. Command.

The leadership lessons of power, precision and presence that no MBA will teach you. Drawn from lived experience, not LinkedIn theory, and unapologetically built for those who lead from the edge—because control without clarity is theatre, and power without consent is collapse.

Published by: Manolutions Publishing
ISBN: 978-1-923621-04-6 (Paperback)
Also available on Amazon Kindle

EVOLVE OR BE REMEMBERED

The Decline of Obedience, the Rise of Intelligence, and the Future of Freedom

This is the wake-up call. A scalpel-sharp lens on AI, sovereignty, obedience, and the species-wide choice we face: transcend or be outgrown. Swallow what your fed, or step off the stage and decentralise your own damn mind.

Published by: Manolutions Publishing
ISBN: 978-1-923621-03-9 (Paperback)
Also available on Amazon Kindle

UNDERSTANDING Y

(*Contributing Author*)

A real-world unpacking of Gen Y — how they think, work, and what they expect from leadership.

Published by: Wiley
ISBN: 978-0-730312-21-5 (Paperback)
Also available on Amazon Kindle

Explore the full catalogue of Manolutions Publishing titles: https://books.manolutions.com

www.ingramcontent.com/pod-product-compliance
Ingram Content Group UK Ltd.
Pitfield, Milton Keynes, MK11 3LW, UK
UKHW050311121225
465828UK00010B/20

9 781923 621008